Sorbets!
by Jim Tarantino

Specialty Cookbook Series Edited by Andrea Chesman

The Crossing Press, Freedom, California 95019

To Ellen

Copyright © 1988 by Jim Tarantino
Cover illustration & design by Betsy Bayley
Text illustration & design by Betsy Bayley
Printed in the U.S.A.

Library of Congress Cataloging-in-Publication Data

Tarantino, Jim.
    Sorbets!

    (Specialty cookbook series)
    Includes index.
    1. Ice cream, ices, etc. I. Title. II. Series.
TX795.T245   1988   641.8'63   88-1198
ISBN 0-89594-270-4
ISBN 0-89594-269-0 (pbk.)

Contents

ACKNOWLEDGMENTS

If someone were to ask, "What are the most important ingredients in your cookbook?" I'd have to answer, "People." Without them, this cookbook would still be just an idea.

First I'd like to thank my wife, Ellen, to whom I dedicate this book, for her support and her help with shopping, tasting, cleaning up spills, and, above all, for her patience with late-night recipe testing and midnight oil burning.

I'd also like to thank Nancy Marcus of the Cookbook Stall in Reading Terminal, who tired of my carping about the lack of decent sorbet recipes and suggested I do something about it; Holly Moore, for his help with word processing, which gave me much more time with food processing; Rick and Libby Frantz, for their microwave tips; Ed Barranco of the Chef's Market, for his help with tracking down exotic fruit; Nahum Waxman of Kitchen Arts and Letters; Joan Santoleri of the Diabetic Treatment Center in Montgomery Hospital; Krista Butvydas; Blanche Schlessinger; Sam Gugino; and, especially, Andrea Chesman, my editor.

I'd really like to thank all the chefs who sent their recipes.

And finally to all my wonderful friends, neighbors, and family who raved when the recipes worked, and gently told me "Well... that's different," when they didn't: Thanks gang!

1
ABOUT SORBETS

A second Ice Age has arrived. Amid the volcanic eruptions of several hot cuisines—Cajun, Tex-Mex, and Thai, to name a few—ice is beginning to form on the palates of cooks and diners alike.

In restaurants, making flavored ices, or sorbets, is becoming as much a daily function as making sauces. And the sorbets being made are becoming an excuse for some of the most imaginative culinary icecapades ever created. Traditional flavors, such as mango and blueberry, are finding themselves in the same company with sorbets of lavender, apple-basil, and cantaloupe-anisette.

Most of the flavored ices in this book are either sorbets or granitas. A sorbet is basically a mixture of a frozen fruit puree and a sugar syrup, sometimes with the addition of a liquor. The word *sorbet* translates from the French to mean sherbet, and it's still used in some cases to describe ices that include a beaten egg white. But if you were to check the frozen food section of your supermarket for sherbet, what you would find is an Americanized version that replaces the egg white with milk or cream.

The word *granita* comes from the Italian word meaning grain. Granitas are a frosty combination of fruits, ice, and sometimes a sweetener. Granitas have a granular texture that's similar to chipped ice. They are also called *granités*.

The idea of flavored ice isn't new. It's likely that a Neanderthal gourmand, after first discovering fire, realized that he could also melt ice, producing what was probably the first sorbet, flavored with a delightful essence of fern and woolly mammoth. Alexander the Great was known to have indulged in a cache of flavored snow after a hard day of sacking Persia. In fact, an early form of granita is attributed to Nero who, during the first century A.D., had runners along the Appian Way pass buckets of snow hand over hand from the mountains to his banquet hall, where it was then mixed with fruit and honey.

Evidence of flavored ices also turned up in the cuisine of the Chinese. Marco Polo returned from the Orient raving about a sherbet-like mixture of frozen fruit and milk, which was an instant hit among the Italians. The seventeenth-century "catering companies" of either Francisco Procopio or Catherine de Medici were responsible for exporting a flavored ice called *sorbetto* to the French. By the end of the seventeenth century, ices and sherbets hit the streets of Paris and spread to England and the rest of Europe where they were enjoyed by commoners and courtiers alike.

The French are responsible for the culinary tradition of using sorbets as palate cleansers. Dishes of flavored ice were served during the middle of the meal as a break in the procession of entrées and the heavy sauces accompanying them.

Today we are practically surrounded by flavored ices. For example, snow cones and water ices (popular at amusement parks and carnivals) are actually variations of an Asian dessert called *sharbat*, a concoction of shaved ice drenched with a sweet flavored syrup. Frozen daiquiris, Popsicles, and even that slushy mixture from water-ice machines found in 24-hour convenience stores are really variations of sorbets.

Sorbets are gaining in appeal for a lot of reasons. Lighter than ice cream due to the absence of milk solids and egg yolks, sorbets have little or no cholesterol and a lower calorie count. Moreover, many interesting recipes can be made with no sugar.

But aside from their dietary appeal, sorbets are elegant. They mark a meal as something special with just the right hint of culinary glamour. The arrival of a sorbet within a meal can be a real ice breaker in more ways than one, stirring up dining chatter with questions as to what it is and compliments as to how good it tastes.

Sorbets can also act as traffic lights to signal the change from white wine to red. They can form the basis of a cool summer cocktail or be served in miniature cups as an hors d'oeuvre. Nowadays sorbets are found practically everywhere within a meal. Depending on when and with what it's served, a sorbet can highlight, contrast, and complement dishes.

But the most remarkable feature about sorbets is their ability to capture a wide array of flavors. They can amplify subtle fragrances, such as lavender or rose, and harness punchy herbs, such as rosemary or saffron, to produce an exquisite blend of spice and ice. Those flavors are what this book is all about.

Food matches in the recipe introductions are simply suggestions as to what dishes a sorbet might be served with. If a particular ice goes well with a spicy Mexican dish, it should go well with any heavily spiced dish. You shouldn't feel that a sorbet recipe will work only with a particular food match. A chart at the end of this chapter provides further suggestions for serving specific sorbets.

Today's cooks place great importance on how a dish works visually, and one aspect of sorbets is their different colors, which range from soft pastels to bright, vibrant hues. Included with each recipe is its corresponding color. This should enable you to think creatively about possible color and flavor combinations. You'll also begin to see that most people initially eat with their eyes. And that's when the fun begins. Sit back and enjoy the double takes when what looks like a creamy lime sherbet is actually a kiwi sorbet. A strawberry sherbet may be a pomegranate-cognac sorbet; an orange ice may be a mango sorbet.

Sorbets as Palate Cleansers

While we're anticipating our first mouth-watering bite at the beginning of a meal, our salivary glands kick into operation and our mouths begin something like a rinse cycle. The gastric juices released also can be stimulated by the acid present in wine, vinegar (tannic acid), or the citric acid in fruits. This process is actually known as whetting one's appetite. Throughout the meal we slowly become satiated, and the flow of gastric juices is reduced. At the same time, the oils present within the various food elements, such as cream sauces and salad dressings, begin to coat the surface of our tongues. Although you may not seem to have any problems distinguishing the subtle seasonings of what you eat, it's your nose that's feeding you most of the information, not your tongue. Your sense of smell is going full steam ahead while the sensations of taste are lagging behind. Now here's where sorbets earn their keep as palate cleansers.

Eat a spoonful of sorbet and the first sensation you experience (the most obvious one) is coolness. The sorbet is not so cold that you feel it with your teeth, but cool enough to lower the temperature of your mouth. (In a physical sense, a sorbet lies midway between ice and liquid, and because of its higher freezing point, its texture is less solid and even feels lighter than ice cream.) The sorbet then begins to cleanse the palate by rinsing the surface of the tongue. The tart citric acids of the fruit in the sorbet will also cause gastric juices to flow. Now your mouth feels refreshed enough to start tasting again.

Basic Components of Sorbets

Sugar Syrups. A sugar syrup is to a sorbet as a stock is to a sauce. The syrup is the foundation that actually binds a sorbet together. And it's responsible for giving a sorbet its snow-like texture.

Surprisingly enough, the primary function of a syrup is not to sweeten a sorbet (which it does), but to aid in the freezing process. Here's what happens.

Sugar syrup, also known as simple syrup, *sirop léger*, or light syrup, is made from boiling granulated sugar and water together just long enough to dissolve the sugar and create a clear syrup. The higher the sugar to water ratio, the heavier the syrup. The heavier the syrup, the longer it takes to freeze, and, in most cases, the smoother the sorbet.

The syrup lowers the freezing temperature of water or juices from 32° F. to 27° F. and keeps the sorbet from turning into a solid ice block. A bottle of cola, for example, with a much higher sugar ratio than even the sweetest sorbet, will freeze at about 16° F. In effect, the sugar syrup acts as chemical chaperon between the fruit puree and ice crystals. It does everything it can to keep these two elements from combining. A ready-to-serve sorbet consist of ice crystals of water, air cells, frozen elements of fruit, and liquid containing sugar. So you see sorbets are never really frozen but are a combination of frozen liquid, air, and solids.

How Much Sugar? The rule of thumb is the less sugar one uses, the higher the freezing temperature and the colder or grainier the sorbet. The greater the sugar density, the longer it takes to freeze and, in some cases, the smoother the sorbet. Successful sorbets can be made without using any sugar at all, as the chapter on Pure Fruit Ices will show you. Sugar syrups should be adapted to the amount of sweetness present in the flavors you are working with. The quantity of sugar in each of the recipes in this book is based on the anticipated sweetness of the mixture.

Preparing Sugar Syrups. Sugar to water ratios will vary in the recipes, but let's take a typical combination of 2 cups of water to 1 cup of sugar to use as an example. In a noncorrosive (ie., stainless steel or enamel) pot, combine the water and sugar and bring to a boil. The solution is finished when it appears to be clear with faint hints of yellow straw color. Avoid boiling for more than 5 minutes as the water will begin to evaporate and your sugar solution will become too heavy. If the solution becomes tan and cloudy, it is starting to caramelize and you've boiled it for too long. Throw it out and start over.

To prepare a sugar syrup in a microwave, combine the water and sugar and stir in a microwave-safe bowl. Heat at 100 percent power until the sugar dissolves (about 3 minutes), then stir again to dissolve any sugar crystals.

The sugar syrup should be at refrigerator temperature to make a good sorbet. If a syrup is too hot, it will cook the fruit puree and change its flavor. Also a warm syrup will lengthen the freezing time of the sorbet, and the texture of the sorbet may become watery or too syrupy.

Syrups stored in the refrigerator will last as long as 9 to 12 months.

Citrus. A good sorbet, like a fine wine, should have a balance of flavors. To counteract the sweetness of the syrup, fresh citrus juices—usually lemon, lime, or orange—are added. Citric acid also aids palate cleansing. Although most fruit contains some level of citric or tannic acid, it is not enough in most cases to offset the amount of sugar in the syrup.

It's absolutely essential that when the recipe calls for lemon or lime juice you use freshly squeezed juices, not bottled.

Of all the citrus fruits, lemon is the most neutral and probably the best to use with the majority of sorbets. Lime, on the other hand, can tame the most strongly flavored ingredients and bring them down to a more palatable level, but it will add its own distinctive flavor. Orange is sweeter and more recognizable in flavor than lemon; it needs to be used in larger quantities to pack the same citric punch as lemon or lime. Freshly squeezed orange juice can be used in most savory sorbets to smooth out the puree.

Equipment

The ease of making sorbets lies not in the kind of ice maker you are using, but in the tools you use to get to that stage. Stainless steel, enamel, and glass cookware are recommended because they are easy to clean, will not readily absorb food odors, and do not interact with acid foods. Copper and aluminum pots should be avoided because they interact with certain types of acidic fruit and wine to produce off flavors. Essentially, the only equipment you really need to make a sorbet is a freezing container and a wire whisk to stir your mixture.

Blenders or Food Processors. You can take advantage of food processors and blenders in two ways. They are great for pureeing tough, fibrous foods, such as apples, pineapples, and carrots; they can also be used for the more delicate fruits and vegetables, but care must be taken to avoid liquefying them. And they can be used in the actual making of sorbets and granitas.

Electric Mixers. If you don't own a food processor or blender, no need to worry. You can puree most fruits and vegetables with an electric mixer and a good kitchen knife in two simple steps. First, finely dice the fruit and put it in a mixing bowl. Then add ¼ cup of juice or syrup to the mixing bowl. Beat, building up speed gradually, until you have a smooth consistency. Then strain through a fine sieve and proceed with the rest of your recipe. If you happen to be working with juicy berries or fruit, you won't have to dice the fruit first.

Food Mills. A hand-cranked stainless steel food mill with three interchangeable disks is arguably one of the more versatile utensils you'll ever use in making sorbets. The turning of the handle of the food mill rotates a blade that presses the fruit against a disk, thereby removing seeds, straining skins, and turning tough and fibrous fruits into a velvety smooth puree. Its biggest advantage is the amount of control it allows you in determining the texture of fruit purees.

Food mills come in 1-quart to 3-quart sizes, with the 1-quart size being more than adequate for the recipes in this book. Look for food mills that have rubber hooks to clamp onto bowls for stability.

Glass Measuring Cups. You'll need at least two. The 1-cup size is great for measuring small amounts of citrus juices and the 4-cup size is particularly useful to place under a food mill and for steeping teas.

Juice Reamer. Preferably use a glass one with curved ridges. It should have a capacity of at least 1 cup.

Strainers and Sieves. There are a number of types of strainers, ranging from mesh skimmers to drum sieves, that will work well in pureeing and straining fruit for making sorbets. Even a cheesecloth is good for straining grapes and berries. The rule of thumb is that the finer the mesh, the smoother the puree. Again, stainless steel is the material of choice.

Freezing Containers. If you are making sorbets without an ice cream machine, you'll need freezing containers. Here's some hints on what to look for. The more surface that's exposed, the faster the freezing process. This makes cake pans and sheet pans excellent choices. Choose either 8-inch to 10-inch round cake pans (at least 2 inches deep) or 9-inch by 13-inch by

2-inch sheet pans. The deeper the pan, the easier it is to stir during the freezing process. Nonaluminum ice cube trays with removable dividers are the next choice; you'll need at least two per recipe. Avoid glass containers because liquid expands as it freezes. See the section on storage (page 16) for additional information on containers.

Ice Cream Makers. If you are really serious about your ices, chances are you may consider buying an ice cream maker. The advantage of an ice cream machine is that it can make a smooth sorbet within an hour. The recipes in this book will work well with all ice makers with a 1-quart (4-cup) capacity.

There are so many machines on the market, with prices ranging from under 50 dollars to several hundred dollars, that it is impossible to rate the best machines for sorbets. *Cook's Magazine* and *Consumer Reports* both provide reliable testing of kitchen equipment and should be consulted for brand name recommendations.

Methods

Now comes the easy part. If you can boil water you can make sorbets. Here are a couple of methods to get you on your way.

Stir Freezing Method. If you don't have an ice cream machine or if you want to make more than one sorbet simultaneously, begin by pouring your sorbet mixture into a freezer container, cover, and let it freeze in the freezer compartment of your refrigerator until the mixture forms a 1-inch to 2-inch frame of ice around the inside of the pan. This will take 1½ to 2 hours. Remove the sorbet from the freezer, scrape the ice from the sides of the container, and stir with a whisk. Or pour into a mixer bowl and use an electric mixer to break up the ice crystals and to incorporate air into the mixture. Return to the freezer for 30 to 50 minutes and repeat the process. You may have to repeat the process 1 to 2 more times, depending on the type of ingredients used, the temperature of freezer, and the desired smoothness of the sorbet, but the amount of freezing time between steps will be briefer. The sorbet is finished when it has the consistency of day-old snow; that is, when you are able to form it or scoop it into a shape. If you intend to serve the sorbet later that day, repeat the stirring process about once every couple of hours to keep it from hardening. Although this process seems long, it's not. The actual time you spend at each interval is only minutes.

Blender/Food Processor Method. When time is of the essence, and you don't have an ice cream machine, this is one of the best ways to produce an ice. Reserve ¼ to ½ cup of your sorbet mixture, cover, and place in your refrigerator. Pour the remaining mixture into 2 ice cube trays with compartments and freeze the mixture until solid, about 4 hours. Meanwhile, place the blender container or food processor bowl along with their steel blades in your freezer. You'll want these items as cold as possible to prevent the sorbet from melting. When the mixture is frozen, combine the frozen sorbet cubes with a small amount of the reserved mixture in the chilled blender or food processor and break up the cubes in small batches. Spoon the sorbet into a storage container and return the mixture to your freezer for at least 30 minutes before serving.

Ice Cream Machines. Your ice cream maker will have complete instructions for making sorbets included in its instruction booklet. Follow the manufacturer's directions.

Storage

In some classic French restaurants, sorbets are served from a dessert trolley in tall, shimmering stainless steel canisters called *sorbetières*. Inside sorbetières are pre-chilled ring-shaped containers which help to keep a sorbet at just the right serving texture. How you store your just-made ices will have as much effect on the taste and texture of your sorbets as the ingredients. Ideally, sorbets taste best when freshly made. If you make sorbets a day or two in advance, here are some important tips on how to store your ices.

Freezers. The best place to store your sorbets is in the freezer compartment of your refrigerator. Free-standing and chest freezers are much too cold. Does too cold a freezer really affect the texture of a sorbet? Yes, a finished sorbet has a firm texture that can be easily scooped with a spoon. That texture hardens when placed in a refrigerator freezer overnight. You can bring the sorbet to serving consistency by placing it in the refrigerator for an hour before you serve it. But if you place a sorbet in a free-standing or chest freezer (with a freezing temperature of 0° F. or below) overnight, the sorbet will freeze rock solid. It will take longer to bring the ice to serving consistency. Since most mixtures defrost from the outside in, what you'll have will be a sorbet that has soft sides and a hard middle. (When that happens, your best bet is to break up the frozen mixture in a food processor or blender and refreeze it to serving consistency as described in the stir freezing method above.)

The ideal freezing temperature is between 10° F. to 20° F., which is the range of most refrigerator freezer compartments. Although 32° F. will make ice cubes, it's not cold enough to make or keep sorbets. By using a freezer thermometer you can determine which part of your freezer is the coldest, or you can adjust the temperature control accordingly to maintain the best freezing environment.

Freezing Containers. I cannot emphasize enough the need for transferring your freshly made sorbets into tightly sealed containers for storage. Improperly sealed containers will cause the flavor of your sorbet to diminish. The sorbet will also pick up other odors, as well as form large ice crystals in the freezer.

The shape of your container is important. Upright plastic containers are good choices. Deli or take-out containers (with a 2-cup or 4-cup capacity) can also be used. Just be sure they're thoroughly cleaned or you may have an ice with hints of the previous night's dinner. Low, flat containers will make your sorbet easier to stir while it freezes, but keeping the finished ice in one is not a great idea. The increased surface area exposes the sorbet to greater amounts of large ice crystals.

To properly store your sorbet and to keep it free of crystals, pack it tightly in your container and cover the surface with a double layer of plastic wrap, leaving no surface area exposed. Then cover with a tight-fitting lid.

How long can a sorbet hold its flavor in a freezer? It depends primarily on the ingredients. Fruit ices are good for about a week. It's not that you won't be able to recognize the flavor after that, but it won't be as intense as if it were freshly made. The flavors of sorbet recipes in the chapters Fruit Sorbets and Pure Fruit Ices diminish rapidly after 2 or more weeks. The recipes in Spirited Sorbets and Pantry Sorbets will hold their flavor a little longer, usually 2 to 3 weeks, before the ices become syrupy and begin to separate.

Bringing a Sorbet to Serving Temperature. To soften a sorbet to serving consistency, use either your refrigerator or a microwave oven. Here are some guidelines and times for different types of ices.

The recipes in the chapters Fruit Sorbets

and Sorbets from the Garden will take between 1 hour to less than 1½ hours to soften in the refrigerator. Spirited Sorbets and sorbets that use alcohol instead of sugar syrup will take 45 to 60 minutes. Since Pure Fruit Ices are made without a sugar syrup or alcohol, they will be a little trickier. The refrigerator time is at least 1½ hours to 2 hours, but you may need to break up the ice in a blender, food processor, or mixer to a smooth, even consistency and then refreeze again for about 30 minutes before serving.

A microwave oven can be very handy for bringing sorbets to serving texture. Remove the sorbet from your freezer and place it, covered, in your microwave. Heat Fruit Sorbets and Sorbets from the Garden at 100 percent power for 60 seconds. Check the texture and repeat (if necessary) with 15-second intervals at 100 percent power until you get your desired consistency. You shouldn't have to repeat that process more than twice. Pure Fruit Ices will need at least 1½ minutes at 100 percent power. Spirited Sorbets will need only 45 seconds. Again check the texture; reheat with intervals of 15 seconds at 100 percent power, if needed. When you can easily form the sorbets into scoops, it's ready to serve.

Sorbets to Go. Sorbets have an out-of-freezer life span of less than 20 to 30 minutes before they start to become too slushy or liquid. But what do you do when you want to bring a fresh batch of sorbets to a potluck dinner or when you want to have some refreshing ices at an open-air concert or a picnic? Here's one solution that will keep your sorbets alive and well for up to 4 to 5 hours outside of your freezer.

What you will need is a small picnic cooler, 8 to 10 pounds of cracked or crushed ice (1 tray of ice cubes = 1 pound of ice), 1 cup kosher salt or sea salt, and some jars with tight-fitting lids (airtight canning jars are perfect for this).

First create a brine by mixing the ice, salt, and 1 cup water in the picnic cooler. Fill the jars with sorbet, leaving about ½ inch of space at the top. Cover the openings with double layers of plastic wrap, with enough overlap to secure them *tightly* with a rubber band. Cover the jars with their lids and place them in the brine. The brine should come up to lid level. If the brine becomes too liquid, simply add more ice.

To serve your ice at the appropriate time, remove the jar from the brine, wipe the lid with a dry towel, carefully remove the plastic wrap, serve, and enjoy.

Troubleshooting

Taste your recipe as you go along. If a sorbet has too much sugar, your tongue will feel it on the tip. Your mouth will feel more thirsty than refreshed—like the effect you may get when you drink a bottle of cola. Too much citrus will cause sensations on the side of your tongue and puckering of your mouth. Some sorbets made from pomegranate, lemon, or other citrus fruits will do this anyway, but you want to be able to control that effect and use it with the best possible food match. Too much sugar and citrus together will suppress the flavor.

The majority of problems that you're likely to encounter with texture will be due to problems in the freezing process. Here's a list of some typical ones.

Problem: Sorbet is grainy with ice crystals.
Solution: Partially defrost the sorbet. Beat 1 egg white until stiff, fold into the sorbet, and begin the freezing process again.

Problem: Sorbet contains large chunks of ice.

Solution: Not enough air has been incorporated into the mixture. Beat the mixture until slushy in a blender, food processor, or heavy-duty mixer and begin the freezing process again.

Problem: Sorbet is almost rock solid and difficult to scoop.
Solution: The sorbet has been kept in the freezer for too long. See the section on bringing sorbets to room temperature on page 17.

Problem: Sorbet is light and powdery.
Solution: The sorbet may lack enough syrup to complete the freezing process. Partially defrost and add ¼ to ½ cup of syrup (or fruit juice if it's a non-sugar recipe) and start the freezing process over.

Problem: Sorbet is runny.
Solution: Is your freezer cold enough? You need a freezing temperature of 27° F. or lower to make a sorbet. If you are using a hand-cranked ice maker, the freezing container may not be cold enough. Hint: When serving ices during the summer or from a hot kitchen, chill a tray of bowls or glasses in the freezer beforehand, add the sorbet, and return them to the freezer. Then serve the sorbet directly from the freezer. Under the best conditions, sorbets will last about 15 to 20 minutes before they liquefy.

Problem: Sorbet is too syrupy or creamy.
Solution: There may be too much sugar in the syrup recipe, or you may have overcooked your fruit.

Check the sugar to water ratio in
your syrup and adjust the recipe
with ¼ cup to ½ cup water.
Also the sorbet could be old.
They last about week or two in
the freezer before they start to
separate and begin to lose flavor
intensity.

Serving Suggestions

Use this table to help you plan your menus with sorbets. These are are only suggestions,
however, and in many instances, it is just a matter of personal preference whether to serve
a sorbet as a palate cleanser or first course dish.

Sorbets	Palate Cleanser	First Course	Dessert
Apple	•		•
Apple Cider Granita	•		•
Apple-Currant Ice	•		•
Avocado		•	
Banana Rum			•
Banana-Strawberry Ice			•
Bellini Ice			•
Blueberry Kiwi Ice	•		•

Sorbets	Palate Cleanser	First Course	Dessert
Blueberry Mint	•		•
Calvados			•
Cantaloupe-Anisette	•	•	
Cantaloupe Champagne		•	•
Carrot Orange		•	•
Chamomile Ice	•		
Champagne	•		•
Chardonnay Granita	•		
Cherimoya			•
Cherry			•
Coconut Galliano			•
Coconut-Papaya		•	•
Concord Grape			•
Cranberry	•		•
Cranberry Apple Ice		•	•
Cucumber Melon Ice	•	•	
Cucumber Mint	•	•	
Dill	•		
Dried Apricot			•
Dried Rose Petal	•	•	
Espresso Granita			•
Feijoa	•		•

Sorbets	Palate Cleanser	First Course	Dessert
Fennel-Anisette		•	
Fresh Fig	•	•	•
Gin	•		
Ginger	•		•
Ginger-Fig Ice		•	•
Gold Gazpacho		•	
Granité Vin Rouge	•		
Grape-Lime Ice	•	•	
Grapefruit Mimosa	•	•	
Grapefruit-Mint	•		
Grapefruit-Vermouth	•	•	
Guinness-Lime	•		
Herb Tea Granita	•		
Hibiscus	•	•	
Italian Water Ice			•
Kiwi			•
Lavender	•	•	
Lemon	•		•
Lemon Grass	•		
Litchi			•
Mango	•		•
Mango Chutney	•	•	

Sorbets	Palate Cleanser	First Course	Dessert
Mango Daiquiri			•
Mango Raspberry Ice			•
Mango Sharbat			•
Margarita-Jalapeño	•		
Marmalade			•
Marsala			•
Melon	•	•	
Midori	•	•	•
Minted Lime	•		
Nectarine-Rosé	•	•	•
Orange	•		•
Orange Dondurma	•		
Orange Spice	•		
Papaya	•		•
Papaya-Passion Fruit Ice	•		•
Passion Fruit			•
Peach	•		•
Pear	•		•
Persimmon	•		
Piña Colada Ice	•	•	•
Pineapple	•		•
Pineapple Cilantro Ice	•	•	

Sorbets	Palate Cleanser	First Course	Dessert
Pineapple Citrus Ice	•	•	
Plum	•		•
Poire William			•
Pomegranate-Cognac	•		
Prickly Pear	•		
Prickly Pear-Banana Ice			•
Prune Plum			•
Pumpkin			•
Quince	•		
Raspberry	•		•
Raspberry Granita	•		•
Raspberry-Peach Ice			•
Red Zinger	•		
Rhubarb			•
Rose Petal	•	•	
Rosemary	•		
Saffron	•		
Sage	•		
Sherry	•	•	•
Sour Cherry Sharbat			•
Star Fruit	•		•
Strawberry			•

Sorbets	Palate Cleanser	First Course	Dessert
Strawberry-Watermelon Ice	●		●
Tamarillo	●	●	
Tarragon	●		
Tequila Lime	●		●
Tomato Ginger		●	
Violet	●	●	
Vodka Lemon	●		
Watermelon-Cassis			●
White Chocolate			●
White Wine Spoom			●

2
FRUIT SORBETS

The most basic of all sorbets are the ones that are made from fruit. The rewards of making fruit sorbets are instant. You get taste up front, and color, color, and more color. One spoonful and you're refreshed.

Fruit sorbets look beautiful arranged on a plate with slices of fresh fruit and berries. Oval dollops of fruit ices sharing a plate with fruit compotes is one of the easiest and most mouth-watering presentations one can make.

With the exception of citrus, all fruits should be strained before you start the freezing process in order to insure some degree of consistency and smoothness. Use noncorrosive materials, such as stainless steel, for straining.

One thing to note is that fruit will darken quickly after it's been pureed, but adding a tablespoon of fresh lemon juice to the puree will hold the color a little longer. And speaking of color, fruit will lighten quite a bit when frozen. For example, the deep green pulp of a fresh kiwi will change to a light green in its sorbet.

When there is a lot of liquid or juice in a fruit puree, an egg white, beaten until stiff, is added to decrease the number of ice crystals formed during the freezing process.

Alcoholic spirits in these recipes are used to enhance the flavor. They are optional, but a good idea in the event that you're working with fruit that is underripe. Partially ripened fruit lacks some of the natural sugar (fructose) that fully ripened fruit contains. The addition of alcohol aids in the freezing process by picking up where the partially ripened fruit leaves off. You can reduce the amount of alcohol but keep the flavor by heating the spirits and then flaming it with a match before adding it to the sorbet. You can also substitute 2 tablespoons of any fruit preserves dissolved in your syrup mixture for the liqueur, should you wish to avoid any alcoholic ingredients.

For some additional fruit combinations look at the recipes in chapter 4, Pure Fruit Ices.

Exotic Fruit

We're in the midst of a phenomenon known as the global pantry. All across America exotic fruits and vegetables, as well as ethnic and regional ingredients, are available. The refrigerated jet has replaced the neighborhood pushcart as a means of bringing a variety of fresh produce to our tables. The choices range from tropical fruit to fresh wild forest mushrooms. But one of the more frequently asked questions in produce aisles seems to be: "What do I do with this?"

Discovering and buying exotic fruit can be as exciting as a jungle safari and almost as perilous. Exotic fruits that look like their domestic counterparts may not play by the same rules when it comes to taste and ripeness. For example, a quince has the same skin color as a pear and even looks the same when you cut one open. But don't try biting into a raw one. Persimmons and passion fruit may look and feel ripe like plums, but they really need to wrinkle before they are of any use to you. Most exotic fruits are picked before they are vine ripened so that they're able to make the trip to the distributor. So check with your produce manager for ripening times.

Finding exotic fruit can be a real quest. Although all of the fruit used in the following recipes have been found in supermarkets, you're not likely to find more than a few items at any given time. There are a few reasons for this. One is cost. Supermarkets have to buy produce by the case from distributors. Grocery produce managers are reluctant to stock a lot of exotic fruit because they're not really sure how well it will sell. But keep asking. If produce managers know there's an interest, they'll keep stocking exotic fruit. Also, feedback is a nice thing. Go back and tell the produce people what you've done with your fruit. More than likely they'll pass this information along to the next person who asks "What do I do with this?"

Other sources for exotic fruit are specialty stores, such as gourmet food shops, which are more likely to take chances with exotic produce because of their clientele, and ethnic grocery stores. You'll be able to find fresh litchis and lemon grass in Oriental markets and feijoas in some Spanish ones. Also there's probably more exotic fruit that passes through your area than you know about. Some of that fruit will never hit the produce aisles. Here's where to look. Produce distributors will sell directly to restaurants and will break cases to do it. Sometimes you can find a friendly distributor who will be willing to sell what's remaining. Tuesdays and Wednesdays seem to be the best times to call produce distributors to check on what's available, as they're more than likely filling restaurant orders for the coming weekend. Also produce distributors can tell you what's hitting the markets and where.

The exotic fruit sorbet recipes are pretty straightforward to enable you to work primarily with the flavors of the fruits. Keep these exotic fruit sorbets simple the first time out. You can always add additional flavorings or other fruit purees the next time around.

Lemon Sorbet

This easy sorbet does it all. As a palate cleanser, Lemon Sorbet can stand up to any dish. By itself, there's nothing more refreshing.

Peel of 1 lemon, julienned and diced
1 cup water
½ cup sugar
½ cup fresh lemon juice
½ cup mineral water or seltzer
1 egg white, beaten until stiff
⅛-inch-wide strips lemon peel or twists
    to garnish

Yield: 6 servings
Color: Pale yellow

Make a syrup by combining the diced lemon peel with the water and sugar in a noncorrosive saucepan and bring to a boil. Simmer for 5 minutes. Remove from the heat and cool. Combine the syrup, lemon juice, and mineral water or seltzer. Freeze according to one of the methods in chapter 1.

When the ice has frozen to a soft, slushy consistency, fold in the beaten egg white with a rubber spatula. Continue the freezing process until the ice is no longer slushy and has a firm texture.

To serve, form the sorbet in oval scoops with 2 large soup spoons and garnish with strips of lemon peel or lemon twists.

Orange Sorbet

Citrus sorbets are universal palate cleansers. This orange sorbet can be matched with any cuisine, during any season of the year.

1 cup water
½ cup sugar
Peel of 1 orange (white part removed), julienned
2 cups fresh orange juice
2 tablespoons unsweetened orange juice concentrate
1 tablespoon Grand Marnier or other orange liqueur (optional)
6 orange shells (optional)

Yield: 6 servings
Color: Bright yellow

Make a syrup by combining the water, sugar, and orange peel in a noncorrosive saucepan and bring to a boil. Simmer for 5 minutes. Remove from the heat and cool. Discard the orange peel. Combine the syrup, juice, juice concentrate, and liqueur. Freeze according to one of the methods in chapter 1.

To serve, slice about one-third from the top of 6 large smooth-skinned oranges and hollow them out. Pipe the sorbet from a pastry bag fitted with a large star tip. Place each finished ice in the freezer and hold until serving.

Variation

Orange Anisette Sorbet. Replace the Grand Marnier with 2 tablespoons of either anisette or Sambucca. Proceed with the recipe as above.

Grapefruit-Mint Sorbet

What a cooler! But this sorbet is good any time of the year, so don't wait for warm weather to prepare it. Your mouth will get a nice tart feel from the grapefruit and the mint will provide a cooling aftertaste. More of a palate cleanser than a dessert sorbet, this should be served when you want to finish off a salad course that includes a particularly heavy vinaigrette.

1 cup water
½ cup sugar
½ cup fresh mint leaves or ¼ cup dried
2 large pink grapefruits
Additional mint leaves to garnish

Yield: 6 servings
Color: Light green

Make a syrup by combining the water and sugar in a noncorrosive saucepan and bring to a boil. Simmer for 5 minutes. Remove from the heat, add the mint leaves, and steep for 20 to 25 minutes. Strain the syrup and discard the mint. Juice the grapefruits and measure out 1 cup of juice. When the syrup is cool, combine with the grapefruit juice. Freeze according to one of the methods in chapter 1. Garnish with additional mint leaves.

Pineapple Sorbet

Need a tasty breakfast sorbet to awaken your taste buds? This ice will do the trick no matter what time of day. Naturally sweet as well as tart, pineapple sorbets can be part of a tropical fruit platter that opens a meal or ends it.

1 cup water
¼ cup granulated sugar
¼ cup brown sugar
2½ cups chopped pineapple (1 medium-size pineapple)
¼ cup fresh lime juice
1 tablespoon white rum (optional)
Sweet star fruit or kiwi slices to garnish (optional)

Yield: 6 servings
Color: Ivory

Make a syrup by combining the water and sugars in a noncorrosive saucepan and bring to a boil. Simmer for 5 minutes. Remove from the heat and cool. Puree the pineapple in a food processor or blender and strain through a fine sieve. Combine the syrup, pineapple, lime juice, and rum. Freeze according to one of the methods in chapter 1.

Garnish with sliced star fruit or kiwi.

Variation

Piña Colada Sorbet. Substitute 1 cup canned coconut cream for the sugar syrup; do not cook. Combine with the remaining ingredients and proceed as above.

Blueberry Mint Sorbet

Deep blue and so cool. I can't think of a better way to complement a meal of grilled fish or chicken. Serve this sorbet on chilled dessert plates with Blackberry Sorbet and Raspberry Sorbet (page 36). Garnish with fresh berries, sprigs of mint, and lemon curls.

1 cup water
⅓ cup sugar
½ cup fresh mint leaves or 3 tablespoons dried
1 pint fresh blueberries or 1 (10-ounce) package frozen
¼ cup fresh lemon juice
1 tablespoon crème de menthe

Yield: 6 servings
Color: Neon purple

Make a syrup by combining the water and sugar in a noncorrosive saucepan and bring to a boil. Simmer for 5 minutes. Remove from the heat, add the mint, and steep for 15 to 20 minutes. Puree the blueberries in a food processor or blender and strain through a fine sieve. Combine the syrup, blueberry puree, lemon juice, and the crème de menthe. Freeze according to one of the methods in chapter 1.

Raspberry Sorbet

Attention chocolatiers. If there's any one sorbet that can cut through the richest chocolate dessert, it's this one.

If fresh raspberries are unavailable, use frozen, but increase the amount of framboise to 2 tablespoons and decrease the sugar to ¼ cup.

¾ **cup water**
¼ **to** ⅓ **cup sugar**
1 full pint fresh ripe raspberries or 1 (10-ounce) package frozen
½ **teaspoon raspberry vinegar**
¼ **cup fresh lemon juice**
1 to 2 tablespoons framboise or any raspberry liqueur (optional)

Yield: 6 servings
Color: Bright red

Make a syrup by combining the water and sugar in a noncorrosive saucepan and bring to a boil. Simmer for 5 minutes. Remove from the heat and cool. Puree the raspberries in a food processor and strain through a fine sieve to remove the seeds. Combine the syrup, raspberry puree, vinegar, lemon juice, and liqueur. Freeze according to one of the methods in chapter 1.

Variation

Blackberry Sorbet. Substitute blackberries for the raspberries, ½ teaspoon balsamic vinegar for the raspberry vinegar, and 1 tablespoon blackberry brandy for the framboise. Proceed with the recipe as above.

Strawberry Sorbet

What makes this sorbet different is the hint of orange that cuts the sweetness of the strawberries and amplifies its flavor. This is just the sorbet to finish off a light summer luncheon.

1 cup water
⅔ cup sugar
2 pints strawberries
½ cup fresh orange juice
1 tablespoon strawberry liqueur or strawberry brandy (optional)

Yield: 6 to 8 servings
Color: Red

Make a syrup by combining the water and sugar in a noncorrosive saucepan and bring to a boil. Simmer for 5 minutes. Remove from the heat and cool. Rinse and hull the strawberries. Then puree and strain through a fine sieve. Combine the syrup, strawberry puree, orange juice, and liqueur. Freeze according to one of the methods in chapter 1.

Variation

Strawberry Champagne Sorbet. Substitute 2 cups champagne for the water, sugar, and orange juice, and do not cook. Combine with the strawberry puree and proceed with the recipe as above.

Peach Sorbet

One of the nicest things about mid-summer is the abundance of sweet juicy peaches. Try a dollop of this dessert sorbet over fresh raspberries or blackberries in a wine goblet.

1 cup water
½ cup sugar
6 to 8 small (or 4 to 5 large) peaches, peeled
Juice of 1 lemon
1 tablespoon peach brandy or Marsala (optional)

Yield: 6 servings
Color: Peach

Make a syrup by combining the water and sugar in a noncorrosive saucepan and bring to a boil. Then simmer for 5 minutes. Remove from the heat and cool. Puree the peaches in a food mill to yield about 1 cup. Combine the syrup, peach puree, lemon juice, and brandy. Freeze according to one of the methods in chapter 1.

Plum Sorbet

This sorbet is a great palate cleanser after roast duck or roast loin of pork. The special thing about plum sorbets is their color—the skin color of the plum will determine the final color of the sorbet. If you are lucky enough to find yellow Mirabelle plums, this ice will really sparkle.

7 to 8 plums, pitted and quartered
1 cup water
½ cup sugar
¼ cup fresh orange juice
Juice of 1 lemon
1 tablespoon Chambord (optional)
Julienned plum slivers to garnish

Yield: 6 servings
Color: Maroon or yellow, depending on the plum

Combine the plums with the water and sugar in a noncorrosive saucepan and simmer for 15 to 20 minutes. Remove from the heat and cool. Puree the plums with the cooking liquid in a food processor or blender and strain through a fine sieve to remove the skins. Combine the plum puree with the orange juice, lemon juice, and Chambord. Freeze according to one of the methods in chapter 1.

Garnish with the julienned plum. For a nice color contrast, use different colored plums for the garnish.

Variation

Champagne Plum Sorbet. Substitute 1⅓ cups dry champagne for the sugar syrup. Do not cook. Proceed with recipe as above.

Cherry Sorbet

When cherries are in season, your choices run the gamut from sweet Bing and yellow Queen Anne cherries to sour Morello. Be sure to buy cherries with stems attached. Cherries without stems could be an indication of mildew during distribution.

1 cup water
⅓ cup sugar
1½ pounds fresh *pitted* cherries (if fresh cherries are unavailable, substitute canned, but reduce the syrup portion to ½ cup water and 2½ tablespoons sugar)
¼ cup fresh lemon juice
1 tablespoon cherry brandy (optional)
2 tablespoons diced maraschino or brandied cherries (optional)

Yield: 6 servings
Color: Red or yellow, depending on the cherry

Combine the water, sugar, and pitted cherries in a noncorrosive saucepan and bring to a boil. Simmer for 5 minutes. Remove from the heat and cool. Puree the mixture in a food processor or blender and strain through a fine sieve to remove the skins. Combine the cherry mixture, lemon juice, and cherry brandy. Freeze according to one of the methods in chapter 1. Fold in the diced cherries midway through the freezing process.

Variation

Golden Yellow Cherry Sorbet. Steep ½ cup fresh rose petals in the sugar syrup for 10 to 15 minutes, strain the syrup, and cool. Substitute 1½ pounds fresh pitted golden cherries for the red cherries, and proceed with the recipe as above.

Apple Sorbet

Depending on the type of apples you're using, you can position this tempting sorbet as either a palate cleanser or as a dessert ice. Tart Granny Smith apples are a good match with sausage or roast pork, and winesap apples make a nice ending to an autumn dinner.

4 to 5 Granny Smith or winesap apples, cored and quartered
1¼ cups unsweetened apple juice or cider
½ cup water
¼ cup sugar
⅛ teaspoon cinnamon
Juice of 1 lemon

Yield: 6 servings
Color: Light tan

Combine the apples with ¼ cup of the apple juice or cider in a noncorrosive saucepan. Bring to a boil and simmer for 5 minutes. Remove from the heat and cool. Combine the pureed apples, syrup, remaining 1 cup juice or cider, cinnamon, and lemon juice. Freeze according to one of the methods in chapter 1.

Variation

Calvados Currant Sorbet. Soak ¼ cup dried currants in ¼ cup calvados or applejack for 4 hours or overnight. Drain the currants and add to the sorbet mixture before freezing.

Pear Sorbet

If you like to experiment, this is a good ice to work with. It combines well with other fruit purees and herbal essences.

1 cup water
½ cup sugar
3 whole cloves
6 pears (Bartlett or bosc), stemmed and unpeeled (about 2 pounds)
1 tablespoon Poire William, pear brandy, or pear schnapps (optional)
Juice of 1 lemon
3 tablespoons crumbled mild goat cheese or sweet (dolci) gorgonzola to garnish (optional)

Yield: 6 servings
Color: Light peach

Make a syrup by combining the water, sugar, and cloves in a noncorrosive saucepan and bring to a boil. Add the pears and simmer for 15 to 20 minutes, or until soft. Remove from the heat, strain the syrup, and cool. Puree the pears in a food processor or blender. Then strain through a fine sieve. Immediately combine the puree (otherwise it will darken), syrup, Poire William, and lemon juice. Freeze according to one of the methods in chapter 1.

If desired, garnish each serving with 1½ teaspoons of crumbled cheese.

Variation

Pear Rosemary Sorbet. Substitute 1½ cups of the Rosemary Sorbet (page 69) mixture before freezing for the syrup portion (water, sugar, and cloves) of this recipe. Proceed as above.

Cranberry Sorbet

After tasting this tart, delicious sorbet, you won't want to wait until Thanksgiving Day to serve it. The sweetness of the orange balances the tartness of the cranberries. This ice can cut through smoked dishes from the grill, as well as game. For an interesting variation, substitute Grand Marnier for the Chambord and garnish the ice with strips of orange zest.

1½ cups water
½ cup sugar
1 pound fresh or frozen cranberries
½ cup fresh orange juice
¼ cup fresh lemon juice
1 tablespoon Chambord or other
    raspberry liqueur

Yield: 6 servings
Color: Deep red

Make a syrup by combining the water and sugar in a noncorrosive saucepan and bring to a boil. Add the cranberries and orange juice and simmer until the berries burst from their skins, 25 to 30 minutes. Remove from the heat, puree in a food processor, and strain through a fine sieve to remove the skins. Let cool. Then combine the cranberries, lemon juice, and Chambord. Freeze according to one of the methods in chapter 1.

Concord Grape Sorbet

This is the perfect way to introduce people to their first sorbet. The flavor and color is instantly recognizable and brings back memories of Popsicles in the summertime. Try serving this sorbet for dessert in a parfait glass with this sorbet on top, Grapefruit-Mint (page 33) in the middle and a nice floral sorbet, such as Lavender (page 73), on the bottom. The sorbet colors of purple, light green, and soft blue are dazzling.

1 cup water
⅓ cup sugar
1 pound Concord grapes
Juice of ½ lemon

Yield: 6 servings
Color: Purple

Make a syrup by combining the water and sugar in a noncorrosive saucepan and bring to a boil. Simmer for 5 minutes. Crush the grapes in a food processor or blender, then strain through a fine sieve to remove the skins. To have a deeper and richer color, leave the puree in the refrigerator overnight before straining out the grape skins. You should have 1½ cups of grape juice. Combine the syrup, grape juice, and lemon juice. Freeze according to one of the methods in chapter 1.

Variation

Green Grape Sorbet. Substitute 1 pound seedless green grapes for the Concord grapes and proceed with the recipe as above.

Cantaloupe-Anisette Sorbet

This is a marriage made in Naples. The taste of cantaloupe and the licorice flavor of anisette are a great match. This summer sorbet goes nicely with cold Italian dishes.

For a more savory version, stir in 2 tablespoons finely diced prosciutto about midway through the freezing process and serve as a first course sorbet.

1 cup water
½ cup sugar
1 tablespoon anise seeds
½ ripe cantaloupe
¼ cup fresh lemon juice
2 tablespoons anisette (Sambucca, Strega, ouzo, or arrack can be substituted)
Various size melon balls to garnish

Yield: 6 servings
Color: Orange

Make a syrup by combining the water, sugar, and anise seeds in a noncorrosive saucepan and bring to a boil. Simmer for 5 minutes. Remove from the heat and cool. When cool, strain and discard the seeds. Puree the melon in a food processor or blender and strain through a fine sieve. Combine the syrup, melon, lemon juice, and liqueur. Freeze according to one of the methods in chapter 1. Garnish with the melon balls.

Variation

Cantaloupe Sorbet. Omit the anise seeds and liqueur. Proceed with the recipe as above and garnish with tiny melon balls and mint.

Melon Sorbet

This is one of the more dazzling looking ices in the book. The poppy seeds give this ice a unique crunch and the flavors of cantaloupe and honeydew melons complement each other nicely. This recipe is the creation of Chef Cathy Casey of Katz's in Seattle, Washington.

¼ **whole cantaloupe**
1 **cup water**
½ **cup sugar**
3 **cups diced honeydew melon**
⅓ **cup Cointreau or other orange-flavored liqueur**
2 **tablespoons fresh lemon juice**
1 **tablespoon fresh lime juice**
1 **tablespoon poppy seeds**

Yield: 6 to 8 servings
Color: Pale green with orange highlights

With a small melon baller, scoop out the cantaloupe to form tiny melon balls (you should have about ½ cup). Cover a dinner plate with waxed paper or freezer wrap, spread out the cantaloupe balls, and freeze.

Make a syrup by combining the water and sugar in a noncorrosive saucepan and bring to a boil. Then simmer for 5 minutes. Remove from the heat and cool.

Puree the honeydew melon in a food processor or blender. In a noncorrosive saucepan, heat the Cointreau, reduce to ¼ cup, and cool. Combine the sugar syrup, melon puree, lemon and lime juices, Cointreau, and poppy seeds. Freeze according to one of the methods in chapter 1.

When the ice has frozen to a soft, slushy consistency, gently fold in the frozen cantaloupe balls with a rubber spatula. Con-

tinue the freezing process until the ice is no
longer slushy and has a firm texture, then
serve.

Watermelon-Cassis Sorbet

The surprising hint of cassis really heightens the cool watermelon flavor of this sorbet.

½ **cup water**
⅓ **cup sugar**
2 **cups seeded watermelon cut into 1-inch chunks**
¼ **cup fresh lemon juice**
1 **tablespoon crème de cassis**

Yield: 6 to 8 servings
Color: Magenta

Make a syrup by combining the water and sugar in a noncorrosive saucepan and bring to a boil. Simmer for 5 minutes. Remove from the heat and cool. Puree the watermelon in a food processor or blender. Combine the syrup, watermelon puree, lemon juice, and cassis. Freeze according to one of the methods in chapter 1.

Variation

Watermelon-Strawberry Sorbet. Use only 1½ cups watermelon and add 1 cup strawberry puree. Proceed with the recipe as above.

Rhubarb Sorbet

The combination of rhubarb and strawberries makes this sorbet a wonderful way to celebrate the transition of spring into summer.

1 pound rhubarb stalks (leaves removed)
1½ cups water
⅔ cup sugar
1 pint strawberries
2 tablespoons fresh lemon juice
1 tablespoon Grand Marnier or other orange liqueur (optional)
Fresh strawberries and mint to garnish

Yield: 6 servings
Color: Light red

Cut the rhubarb into 1-inch pieces. Combine the rhubarb with the water and sugar in a noncorrosive saucepan and bring to a boil. Reduce the heat and simmer until the rhubarb is tender. Remove the mixture from the heat, strain out the rhubarb solids, and reserve the syrup. Hull and slice the strawberries, combine with the cooked rhubarb, and puree in a food processor or blender. Strain the rhubarb and strawberries through a fine sieve. Combine the fruit puree, cooking liquid, lemon juice, and Grand Marnier. Freeze according to one of the methods in chapter 1. Garnish with slices of fresh strawberries and mint leaves.

Feijoa Sorbet

Feijoa (fay-HO-ah) ice has layers of different flavors that just keep unraveling. These small green melons are about the size of kiwis. Hints of pineapple as well as citrus makes this perfumed dessert sorbet a good match with Papaya Sorbet (page 56) or Mango Sorbet (page 55).

1 cup water
½ cup sugar
1 pound feijoas (7 to 8 small feijoas)
½ banana
1 tablespoon fresh lime juice

Yield: 6 servings
Color: Tan

Make a syrup by combining the water and sugar in a noncorrosive saucepan and bring to a boil. Simmer for 5 minutes. Remove from the heat and cool. Halve the feijoas, scoop out the pulp, and discard the rind. Puree the feijoas with the banana in a food processor or blender and strain through a fine sieve. Combine the syrup, fruit puree, and lime juice. Freeze according to one of the methods in chapter 1.

Cherimoya Sorbet

Cherimoya is an artichoke-shaped fruit with a creamy interior that tastes like a vanilla custard with hints of mango and papaya. When ripe, the green flesh of the cherimoya will turn gray. At that point, use immediately.

Serve this creamy tropical sorbet as a dessert.

1 cup water
½ cup sugar
2 cherimoyas
½ cup fresh orange juice
¼ cup fresh lime juice
Pinch nutmeg
Pinch cardamom

Yield: 6 servings
Color: White

Make a syrup by combining the water and sugar in a noncorrosive saucepan and bring to a boil. Simmer for 5 minutes. Remove from the heat and cool. Split the cherimoya in half, scoop out the pulp, remove the seeds, and puree with the orange juice in a food processor or blender. Strain through a fine sieve. Combine the syrup, fruit puree, lime juice, and spices. Freeze according to one of the methods in chapter 1.

Variation

Atemoya Sorbet. Substitute 2 atemoyas for the cherimoyas and proceed with the recipe as above.

Kiwi Sorbet

Kiwis are available year-round, and its juicy pulp is just begging to be turned into a sorbet. What makes this particular recipe unique is the combination of kiwi and vanilla. Try it in combination with Pomegranate-Cognac Sorbet (page 59) and Mango Sorbet (page 55).

1 cup water
½ cup sugar
1 vanilla bean, split, or 1 teaspoon vanilla extract
8 kiwis
1 tablespoon Cointreau or other orange liqueur (optional)
2 tablespoons fresh lemon juice
Additional kiwi slices to garnish

Yield: 6 servings
Color: Light green

Make a syrup by combining the water, sugar, and vanilla bean (do not add vanilla extract at this time) in a noncorrosive saucepan and bring to a boil. Simmer for 5 minutes. Remove from the heat and cool. Peel the kiwis and puree. Strain the syrup and discard the vanilla bean. Combine the syrup, kiwi puree, lemon juice, and Cointreau (and vanilla extract, if vanilla bean is not used). Freeze according to one of the methods in chapter 1. Garnish with fresh kiwi slices.

Variation

Kiwi Champagne Sorbet. Substitute 1½ cups champagne for the sugar syrup; do not cook. Omit the vanilla. Proceed with the recipe as above.

Prickly Pear Sorbet

The prickly pear, or cactus pear, really does come from cactus plants. Prickly pears are available from early fall through spring. They are picked when their skins are green in color, but they should ripen to a dark yellow or reddish brown before you use them. This sorbet is perfect for cutting through the heat of Tex-Mex and Southwestern cuisine.

⅓ **cup sugar**
1 **cup water**
8 **prickly pears**
½ **cup fresh orange juice**
Juice of 1 whole lemon

Yield: 6 servings
Color: Apricot

Make a syrup by combining the sugar and water in a noncorrosive saucepan and bring to a boil. Simmer for 5 minutes. Slice the prickly pears in half lengthwise, then remove the pulp with a spoon. Remove the seeds by straining through a fine sieve. Combine the syrup, prickly pears, and lemon juice. Freeze according to one of the methods in chapter 1.

Fresh Fig Sorbet

Chef Lisa Borst (member of the American Culinary Foundation) of the Inn at South Newfane in Vermont has the perfect use for overripe fresh figs. She makes them into a sorbet which she serves with salad of duck confit and radicchio. You can also serve this sorbet following a meat course or as a dessert with sliced fresh figs.

1½ pounds ripe figs (purple figs are recommended)
1 tablespoon fresh lemon juice
1¼ teaspoons cinnamon
4 cups water
2 cups granulated sugar
3 egg whites
¼ cup confectioners' sugar

Yield: 6 to 10 servings
Color: Pale rusty violet

Peel and puree the figs in a food processor (this should yield about 2 cups). Over medium heat, reduce the fig puree to 1½ cups. Add the lemon juice and cinnamon.

Make a syrup by combining the water and granulated sugar in a noncorrosive saucepan and bring to a boil. Simmer for 5 minutes. Remove from the heat and cool. Add the puree to the syrup. Freeze according to one of the methods in chapter 1.

Beat the egg whites until firm, then slowly beat in the confectioners' sugar until stiff. When the ice has frozen to a soft, slushy consistency, fold in the beaten egg white with a rubber spatula. Continue the freezing process until the ice is no longer slushy and has a firm texture.

Mango Sorbet

Mangoes show up in three of the world's spiciest cuisines: Mexican, Indian, and Caribbean. And it performs practically the same role in each: to cool and refresh. You can determine when a mango is ripe by its skin color, which turns from reddish green to yellow.

1 cup water
½ cup sugar
2 to 3 mangoes
Juice of 1 lime
Juice of 1 lemon
1 tablespoon white rum (optional)

Yield: 6 servings
Color: Yellow

Make a syrup by combining the water and sugar in a noncorrosive saucepan and bring to a boil. Simmer for 5 minutes. Remove from the heat and cool. Peel and puree the mangoes in a food processor or blender. Strain through a fine sieve. Combine the syrup, mangoes, lime juice, lemon juice, and rum. Freeze according to one of the methods in chapter 1.

Papaya Sorbet

This beautiful bright yellow sorbet works well either as a palate cleanser or a dessert. If papayas are shipped before ripening, they will have a reddish green skin. Wait until they turn bright yellow before you turn one into a sorbet. The skin happens to be quite bitter so make sure that you thoroughly peel the fruit before pureeing. Serve this ice in papaya halves and garnish with strips of lime peel.

1 cup water
½ cup sugar
1 large or 2 small yellow papayas
3 tablespoons fresh lime juice
1 tablespoon white rum (optional)

Yield: 6 servings
Color: Bright yellow

Make a syrup by combining the water and sugar in a noncorrosive saucepan and bring to a boil. Simmer for 5 minutes. Remove from the heat and cool. Peel, seed, and puree the papaya in a food processor. You should have 1 cup of puree. Combine the syrup, papaya, lime juice, and rum. Freeze according to one of the methods in chapter 1.

Passion Fruit Sorbet

Look for dark green fruit from Brazil during the spring and early summer and bright pear-yellow fruit from Florida from fall to mid-winter. Wait until the skin becomes wrinkled, almost like an alligator. Then you know that it's ripe. Serve this sorbet by itself with some good champagne on the side.

1 cup water
½ cup sugar
8 ripe (wrinkled) passion fruit (yields about ½ cup)
½ cup fresh orange juice
¼ cup fresh lemon juice
1 tablespoon fresh lime juice

Yield: 6 servings
Color: Yellow

Make a syrup by combining the water and sugar in a noncorrosive saucepan and bring to a boil. Simmer for 5 minutes. Remove from the heat and cool. Over a noncorrosive saucepan, halve the passion fruit, scoop out the seeds and pulp with a spoon, and add the orange juice to the saucepan. Bring the mixture to a very slow boil, reduce the heat, and simmer for 10 to 15 minutes. Remove from the heat and cool. Strain the mixture and discard the seeds. Combine the mixture with the syrup, lemon juice, and lime juice. Freeze according to one of the methods in chapter 1.

Persimmon Sorbet

Persimmons have a hot orange color and are available from mid-October to December. Choose ones that are fairly soft to the touch.

Let persimmons ripen for at least 3 to 4 days at room temperature. Then, when you think they look and feel ripe, wait 2 more days. The skin should begin to shrivel and appear loose. If patience is an ingredient that happens to be scarce, you can freeze persimmons until they are rock hard and then let them thaw to room temperature (takes about 2 days).

1 cup water
¾ cup brown sugar
4 persimmons
Juice of ½ lemon

Yield: 6 servings
Color: Pale apricot

Make a syrup by combining the water and brown sugar in a noncorrosive saucepan and bring to a boil. Simmer for 5 minutes. Remove from the heat and cool. Remove the stems from fruits and peel. Puree the pulp in a food processor and strain through a fine sieve. Combine the syrup, fruit puree, and lemon juice. Freeze according to one of the methods in chapter 1.

Pomegranate-Cognac Sorbet

Pomegranates start to surface in early fall, but these early fruits tend to be small and will not yield as much juice as those in late fall or early winter. Underripe pomegranates have a yellow interior, where riper ones are a deep cherry red. The heavier the fruit, the more juice it contains. Pomegranates have a long shelf life—more than 3 to 4 weeks. Wait until they are nice and soft before cutting into them. Also, pomegranate juice and seeds freeze well.

1 cup water
⅓ cup sugar
6 pomegranates
Juice of ½ lemon
1 tablespoon cognac

Yield: 6 servings
Color: Red wine

Make a syrup by combining the water and sugar in a noncorrosive saucepan and bring to a boil. Simmer for 5 minutes. Remove from the heat and cool. Carefully cut the pomegranates into quarters. Place a colander over a bowl to collect the pomegranate juice. Hold the pomegranate quarters over the colander and bend back the rinds to release the seeds. Reserve ½ cup of seeds for garnishing and run the remaining seeds through a food mill for additional juices. This should yield about 2 cups. Combine the syrup, pomegranate juice, lemon juice, and cognac. Freeze according to one of the methods in chapter 1. Garnish each individual serving with 1 tablespoon of the reserved seeds.

Quince Sorbet

Quince has become a popular fruit recently, but cooks have been using quinces in stews and pies since Colonial days. Quinces show up in practically every cuisine. You can find them in Alsatian choucroutes, Moroccan lamb stews, and American beef stews. Of course, this sorbet would be nice accompaniment to any of those one-dish meals.

1 cup sugar
2 cups water
3 quinces
Juice of 1 whole lemon
½ cup pink or rosé champagne
  (optional)

Yield: 6 servings
Color: Salmon pink

Make a syrup by combining the water and sugar in a noncorrosive saucepan, bring to a boil, then simmer for 5 minutes. Peel, core, and roughly chop the quinces. Combine them with the sugar syrup and simmer, covered, until the quinces are pink and tender, 45 to 60 minutes. Remove the quinces with a slotted spoon and puree in a food processor. This should yield about 1 cup. Strain the cooking syrup, and combine with the quince puree, lemon juice, and champagne. Freeze according to one of the methods in chapter 1.

Star Fruit Sorbet

Star fruits, or carambolas, sneak in and out of specialty food stores and supermarkets during different times of the year. Look for the ones that are starting to turn from straw green to yellow. Depending on the type of star fruit, you can either have a very tart palate cleanser or a sweet dessert sorbet. Narrow ribs on the fruit indicate a tart fruit that can be a pleasant first course sorbet. Thick white ribs indicate a fruit that's on the sweeter side.

1 cup sugar
2 cups water
5 ripe star fruit
1 tablespoon fresh lemon juice

Yield: 6 servings
Color: Canary yellow

Make a syrup by combining the water and sugar in a noncorrosive saucepan and bring to a boil. Simmer for 5 minutes. Remove from the heat and cool. Slice 4 of the star fruit and puree in a blender or food processor; then strain through a fine sieve to remove the skins. Combine the syrup, star fruit puree, and lemon juice. Freeze according to one of the methods in chapter 1. Garnish with the remaining star fruit cut in ¼-inch slices.

Tamarillo Sorbet

Tamarillo, also called tree tomatoes, are available from late summer to early fall. The colors of these egg-shaped fruits range from yellow to deep red. When ripe, the fruit will give slightly to pressure, like a ripe plum. Tamarillos must be gently cooked to open up their amazing flavor of tomato and fruit. This sorbet can hold up well to a spicy stir fry.

1½ cups water
1 cup sugar
6 tamarillos
Juice of 1 lemon
1 tablespoon Kir or crème de cassis
   (optional)

Yield: 6 servings
Color: Brick red

Make a syrup by combining the water and sugar in a noncorrosive saucepan and bring to a boil. Simmer for 5 minutes. Set aside.

In another pot, bring water to a boil, add the tamarillos a few at a time, and blanch for about 30 seconds; then remove and plunge into ice water. Peel off the skins. Cut the fruit in chunks and simmer gently in the sugar syrup for 30 to 40 minutes. Remove the tamarillos and puree in a food processor or blender. Strain the puree through a fine sieve to remove the seeds. Combine the tamarillos, syrup, lemon juice, and liqueur. Freeze according to one of the methods in chapter 1.

3

SORBETS FROM THE GARDEN

If you have ever tasted the sweetness of vine-ripened tomatoes or freshly picked summer corn, it will come as no surprise that sorbets made from vegetables can be every bit as sweet as fruit sorbets. And their different flavors can bring an added depth and dimension to ices. Sweet fragrances, cool mint, and the tastes of tart savory herbal ices are but some of the sensations that can liven your palate.

Some of the most dazzling presentations can be made with savory sorbets from the garden. Salad-sorbets, highlighted by beautiful arrangements of salad greens, are the best of both worlds. Garden fresh vegetables are complemented by the intense flavors of vegetable and herbal ices. And floral sorbets look positively elegant with garnishes made from extra petals. These are primarily first course sorbets, but they can be used throughout the meal as palate cleansers.

Herbal Sorbets

Herbal sorbets can stand up to anything you put them against. They will instantly bring your palate back to life no matter how heavy the cream sauce or highly seasoned the salad dressing. Herbal ices are particularly good at beating back the heat waves from spicy Tex-Mex and Caribbean dishes.

Prepare fresh herbs by pounding them in a mortar and pestle to release their oils. Steep herbs in just-boiled water as you would teas. After the solution has cooled, strain and start freezing the mixture.

Most of the following recipes will work with dried herbs as well as fresh, but use only half the quantity of herbs the recipe specifies.

If you enjoy experimenting, try using some of the herb-flavored syrups with other sorbets. For example, try making a sorbet using a thyme-flavored sugar syrup with about 1 cup of pear puree. Or steep 1 tablespoon of tarragon in the sugar syrup of the Apple Sorbet on page 41.

Floral Sorbets

The idea of cooking with flowers is centuries old. Recipes for flower cookery have been found in old Roman cookbooks. In practically every culture and cuisine, flowers are pickled, candied, stewed, and fried. Flowers are made into jams and wines, mixed into butter, and even eaten raw in salads. In this chapter you'll find them to be the basis of some exquisite sorbets—both sweet and savory—that combine soft pastel colors with a bouquet of Parisian fragrances.

One of the best sources of flowers are the ones you grow yourself. Like garden-grown tomatoes, garden-fresh flowers taste better than the hot house varieties. The more fragrant the flower, the more flavor you'll be able to extract. Also, the richer the color of the particular petal, the deeper the color of your sorbet. Preparing flowers for sorbets is easy and they follow pretty much the same rules that apply to fruits and vegetables from your garden.

Carefully remove the stems and leaves, and thoroughly wash the flowers before using them. You can store flowers between layers of paper towels in the refrigerator until you are ready to use them. Definitely avoid flowers that have been sprayed with insecticides. Only the pesticides you would use on your vegetables should be used on your flowers. Look for flowers that are just about to bloom. An old flower will not have the same intensity of flavor as a younger one.

Floral sorbets can be garnished with their own candied petals or flowers (see page 166). But don't get carried away, or you may end up with something that looks like a frozen Hawaiian shirt.

Edible Flowers

Not all flowers are edible. If the flower doesn't appear on the list below, then the only place it should appear on your table is in a vase. The following flowers will work well in sorbets or in candied flower petals. Herbal flowers also make nice garnishes for savory sorbets.

Borage blossoms
Carnations
Chive blossoms (for garnishing)
Chrysanthemums
Dandelions
Elderberry blossoms
Gardenias
Lavender blossoms
Lemon, lime, and orange blossoms
Lilacs
Marigolds (marigold petals can work as a substitute for saffron in the Saffron Sorbet, page 113)
Nasturtiums
Pansies (for garnishing and candying)
Roses
Squash and zucchini blossoms (for garnishing)
Violets

Minted Lime Sorbet

The combination of tart lime with the cool mint makes this sorbet a particularly soothing and versatile palate cleanser. In fact, it pairs nicely with spicy or grilled, smoky dishes. And it can really liven up your palate during an elegant winter dinner.

2 cups water
1 cup sugar
½ cup tightly packed fresh mint leaves
  or ¼ cup dried
½ cup fresh lime juice
Grated peel of 1 lime (about 1 teaspoon)
1 tablespoon green crème de menthe
  (optional)
Mint leaves to garnish

Yield: 6 servings
Color: White

Combine the water and sugar in a noncorrosive saucepan and bring to a boil. Then simmer for 5 minutes. Remove from the heat, add the mint leaves, and steep for 15 minutes. Strain the syrup mixture and cool. Combine the syrup, lime juice, lime peel, and crème de menthe. Freeze according to one of the methods in chapter 1. Garnish each serving with extra mint leaves.

Variation

Lemon Balm Sorbet. Substitute lemon balm for the mint, ¼ cup lemon juice for the lime juice, and 2 tablespoons dry vermouth for the crème de menthe. Proceed with the recipe as above.

Dill Sorbet

The lemon and gin in this sorbet is nicely complemented by the burst of dill. Tart and savory sorbets are always good matches for seafood, and this ice is no exception.

1½ **cups water**
¾ **cup sugar**
¼ **cup tightly packed fresh dill sprigs**
½ **cup fresh lemon juice**
¼ **cup gin**
Additional dill sprigs to garnish

Yield: 6 servings
Color: White

Make a syrup by combining the water and sugar in a noncorrosive saucepan and bring to a boil. Simmer for 5 minutes. Remove from the heat and cool. Add the dill and steep for 15 minutes. Strain the syrup. Combine the syrup, lemon juice, and gin. Freeze according to one of the methods in chapter 1. Form each serving into 2 oval scoops. Garnish with sprigs of dill.

Rosemary Sorbet

This ice is assertive enough to fit into any cuisine as a palate cleanser. Try it in combination with the tart Lemon Sorbet (page 31) and the fragrantly sweet Hibiscus Sorbet (page 74).

2 cups water
1 cup sugar
1 lemon
½ cup fresh rosemary leaves or ¼ cup dried

Yield: 6 servings
Color: White

Make a syrup by combining the water and sugar in a noncorrosive saucepan and bring to a boil. Simmer for 5 minutes. Peel the lemon, and julienne the peel into small strips. Combine with the rosemary and steep in the sugar syrup for about 20 minutes. Juice the lemon. Strain the syrup. Combine the syrup and lemon juice. Freeze according to one of the methods in chapter 1. Serve in cognac glasses for a nice presentation.

Sage Sorbet

This ice truly fits the category of a savory sorbet. The first spoonful delivers a burst of fragrant sage, followed by the combined flavors of vermouth and tart lime. This refresher is a great palate cleanser for robust dishes, such as venison or pheasant. It also works well with provincial French, Spanish, and Portuguese one-dish meals. Sage Sorbet is one hardy sorbet that can also be included as part of a salad.

Garnish with sage flowers from your herb garden, if available.

Make a syrup by combining the water and sugar in a noncorrosive saucepan and bring to a boil. Simmer for 5 minutes. Peel the lime and julienne the peel into small strips. Add the lime peel and the sage to the sugar syrup and steep for about 20 minutes. Juice the lime. Strain the syrup. Combine the syrup, lime juice, and vermouth. Freeze according to one of the methods in chapter 1.

1½ cups water
1 cup sugar
1 whole lime
½ cup fresh sage leaves or ¼ cup dried
½ cup dry vermouth

Yield: 6 servings
Color: White

Tarragon Sorbet

This refreshing ice works nicely as a palate soother after spicy appetizers or hors d'oeuvres. It has slight hints of licorice, and the Armagnac seems to complement that nicely.

2 cups mineral water
1 cup sugar
1 lemon
½ cup fresh tarragon leaves or ¼ cup dried
2 tablespoons Armagnac (optional)
1 egg white, beaten until stiff

Yield: 6 servings
Color: White

Make a syrup by combining the water and sugar in a noncorrosive saucepan and bring to a boil. Simmer for 5 minutes. Peel the lemon and julienne the peel into small strips. Add the lemon peel and tarragon to the sugar syrup and steep for about 20 minutes, then strain the syrup and cool. Juice the lemon. Combine the syrup, lemon juice, and Armagnac. Freeze according to one of the methods in chapter 1.

When the ice has frozen to a soft, slushy consistency, fold in the beaten egg white with a rubber spatula. Continue the freezing process until the ice is no longer slushy and has a firm texture. Then serve.

Ginger Sorbet

The flavor of ginger comes across as sweet rather than spicy in this sorbet. And the tartness of the lime balances this ice nicely. This palate-soothing sorbet makes a great complement to a spicy oriental salad.

2 cups water
1 cup sugar
1-inch cube fresh ginger, minced
½ cup fresh lime juice
1 egg white, beaten until stiff

Yield: 6 servings
Color: White

Make a syrup by combining the water and sugar in a noncorrosive saucepan and bring to a boil. Simmer for 5 minutes. Remove from the heat, add the ginger, steep for 15 minutes, and cool. Strain the syrup. Combine the syrup and lime juice. Freeze according to one of the methods in chapter 1.

When the ice has frozen to a soft, slushy consistency, fold in the beaten egg white with a rubber spatula. Continue the freezing process until the ice is no longer slushy and has a firm texture. Then serve.

Lavender Sorbet

This herb has a perfume-like bouquet. It is good served after grilled salmon or swordfish.

2 cups water
1 cup sugar
½ cup lavender sprigs
½ cup fresh lemon juice
**Lavender sprigs and 6 tablespoons
   champagne to garnish**

Yield: 6 servings
Color: White

Make a syrup by combining the water and sugar in a noncorrosive saucepan and bring to a boil. Add ½ cup lavender sprigs and simmer, covered, for 15 to 20 minutes. Remove from the heat, strain, and cool. Combine the syrup and lemon juice. Freeze according to one of the methods in chapter 1.

Serve in champagne saucers garnished with sprigs of lavender and drizzle over each serving 1 tablespoon of champagne.

Hibiscus Sorbet

My first exposure to the real potential of sorbets was tasting a menage à trois that included Hibiscus Sorbet, Rosemary Sorbet (page 69), and Lemon Sorbet (page 31). Hibiscus Sorbet is exquisite by itself, but combined with the other two, this palate cleanser is absolutely sensual.

1 cup water
½ cup sugar
½ cup fresh hibiscus petals or ¼ cup dried
1 cup Moselle wine (preferably an Auslese)
½ cup lemon-scented mineral water
2 tablespoons fresh lemon juice
Fresh hibiscus petals to garnish

Yield: 6 servings
Color: White

Make a syrup by combining the water and sugar in a noncorrosive saucepan and bring to a boil. Simmer for 5 minutes. Remove from the heat, add the hibiscus petals, and steep for 10 to 15 minutes. Strain the syrup and cool. Combine the syrup, wine, mineral water, and lemon juice. Freeze according to one of the methods in chapter 1.

To serve, scoop the sorbet with a melon baller and serve in champagne saucers garnished with fresh hibiscus petals.

Violet Sorbet

Fragrant violets share a long history with food—as far back as ancient Greece and Rome. This sorbet works particularly well following either a white or dark chocolate mousse.

2½ cups water
1 cup sugar
1 orange peel, white pith removed, julienned
4 cloves
1 cinnamon stick
½ vanilla bean, split
1 cup thoroughly washed and dried violet petals
1 tablespoon brandy
Candied violet petals (page 166) to garnish

Yield: 6 servings
Color: Light lavender

Make a syrup by combining the water and sugar in a noncorrosive saucepan and bring to a boil. Add the orange peel, cloves, cinnamon stick, and vanilla bean. Simmer for 15 minutes. Remove the syrup from the heat and strain. Place the violet petals in a glass or ceramic container with a lid (do not use metal), and cover with the strained syrup. Cover the container and let it sit for at least 4 to 5 hours, preferably overnight. Strain the liquid, add the brandy. Freeze according to one of the methods in chapter 1.

Garnish each individual serving with candied violet petals.

Rose Petal Sorbet

The rose is a universal symbol of romance. But don't wait until Valentine's Day for an excuse to try this exquisite sorbet. Just getting through another busy week should be excuse enough. Serve this sorbet in champagne flutes along with a glass of your favorite sparkler.

1 cup water
⅓ cup sugar
1 cup tightly packed fresh red rose petals
1 cup champagne
1 tablespoon rose water (available at specialty stores)
2 tablespoons fresh lemon juice
Candied rose petals (page 166) to garnish

Yield: 6 servings
Color: Pink

Make a syrup by combining the water and sugar in a noncorrosive saucepan and bring to a boil. Simmer for 5 minutes. Remove from the heat, add the rose petals, and steep in the syrup for 15 to 20 minutes, or until the syrup blushes to the color of rosé wine. Strain the syrup and combine with the champagne, rose water, and lemon juice. Freeze according to one of the methods in chapter 1.

Serve in champagne flutes or white wine glasses. Garnish each serving with 1 tablespoon candied petals.

Avocado Sorbet

People are very pleasantly surprised by this fragrant sorbet. The obvious food match would be with a dish from the Southwest, but this sorbet is also nice after a cold pasta salad.

1 cup water
⅔ cup sugar
2 small or 1 large ripe avocado
¼ cup fresh lemon juice
Juice and grated peel of 1 lime
1 tablespoon gold tequila

Yield: 6 servings
Color: Light green

Make a syrup by combining the water and sugar in a noncorrosive saucepan and bring to a boil. Simmer for 5 minutes. Cool. Puree the avocado with ¼ cup of the syrup. Combine the puree, syrup, lemon juice, lime juice and peel, and tequila. Freeze according to one of the methods in chapter 1.

Serving suggestion: Core and separate 2 small Belgian endives and arrange the leaves with Bibb lettuce on 6 individual salad plates. Juice 2 limes and grate the peel. Peel ½ pound jicama and 2 Granny Smith apples and julienne into match sticks. Toss the jicama and apples with the lime juice, the grated lime peel, and 2 tablespoons chopped fresh coriander. Arrange on top of the endive and lettuce. Top with 2 small scoops of sorbet and serve.

Carrot Orange Sorbet

This bright orange sorbet may be sweet enough to end a meal. It's also an attractive way to begin a light dinner.

1 pound fresh carrots, peeled and cut into ½-inch slices
1 cup fresh orange juice
1 cup water
½ cup sugar
1 tablespoon Madeira
1 teaspoon white wine vinegar
2 tablespoons fresh lemon juice

Yield: 6 servings
Color: Orange

In a noncorrosive saucepan, steam the carrots in the orange juice until tender. Puree the carrot mixture in a food processor or blender and strain through a fine sieve.

Make a syrup by combining the water and sugar in a noncorrosive saucepan and bring to a boil. Simmer for 5 minutes. Remove from the heat and cool. Combine the carrot puree, syrup, Madeira, vinegar, and lemon juice. Freeze according to one of the methods in chapter 1.

Fennel-Anisette Sorbet

This licorice-flavored ice holds up nicely with tapas and other tangy hors d'oeuvres. Try pairing this one with the Grapefruit-Vermouth Sorbet (page 88).

1 cup water
⅔ cup sugar
1 fennel bulb with greens
2 tablespoons fresh lemon juice
1 tablespoon anisette, Sambucca, or Strega
Sprigs of fennel greens to garnish

Yield: 6 servings
Color: White with green highlights

Make a syrup by combining the water and sugar in a noncorrosive saucepan and bring to a boil. Simmer for 5 minutes. While the syrup is simmering, remove the greens from the fennel stalk and reserve 1 tablespoon for later use. Remove the syrup from the heat, add the fennel greens, and steep in the syrup for 15 to 20 minutes. Strain and cool.

Puree the fennel bulb in a food processor or blender. Strain the puree through a fine sieve. Combine the syrup, fennel puree, lemon juice, anisette, and the remaining tablespoon of fennel greens. Freeze according to one of the methods in chapter 1. Garnish each individual serving with sprigs of fennel greens.

Cucumber Mint Sorbet

A nice sorbet to follow a salad; it is perfect for cutting through strong salad dressings.

1 cup water
⅔ cup sugar
½ cup fresh mint or 3 tablespoons dried
2 medium-size cucumbers
2 tablespoons fresh lime juice
1 tablespoon crème de menthe (optional)
Mint sprigs to garnish

Yield: 6 servings
Color: Light green

Make a syrup by combining the water and sugar in a noncorrosive saucepan and bring to a boil. Simmer for 5 minutes. Remove from the heat, add the mint, and steep for 15 to 20 minutes. Strain and cool.

Peel and seed the cucumbers and puree in a food processor or blender. Combine the syrup, cucumber puree, lime juice, and crème de menthe. Freeze according to one of the methods in chapter 1. Garnish each individual serving with a sprig of mint.

Tomato Ginger Sorbet

Here's a stunning presentation for this elegant first course sorbet. Arrange Boston or Bibb lettuce on cold salad plates. Make a nest of sprouts and center it on each plate. Then add an oval-shaped scoop of sorbet. The taste of this combination sorbet-salad truly lives up to its looks.

1 cup water
1 cup sugar
2 tablespoons finely chopped crystallized ginger
2 pounds vine-ripened red or plum tomatoes, peeled and seeded
1 teaspoon ground coriander
1 teaspoon sherry vinegar
1 lemon, juice and grated peel

Yield: 6 servings
Color: Red

Combine the water, sugar, and ginger in a noncorrosive saucepan and bring to a boil. Simmer for 5 minutes. Remove from the heat and cool. Puree the tomatoes in a food processor and strain through a fine sieve. Combine the ginger syrup, tomato puree, coriander, sherry vinegar, and lemon peel in a noncorrosive saucepan and simmer for 40 to 50 minutes. Cool and add the lemon juice. Freeze according to one of the methods in chapter 1.

Gold Gazpacho Sorbet

If there's one sorbet that embodies the style of Southwestern cuisine, it's this one. It was inspired by Chef Stephen Pyles of the Routh Street Café in Dallas, Texas.

½ **cup water**
½ **cup sugar**
2 **serrano peppers, sliced in half and seeded**
¼ **cup chopped mango**
¼ **cup chopped papaya**
¼ **cup chopped cantaloupe**
¼ **cup chopped sweet yellow pepper**
⅛ **teaspoon saffron**
3 **yellow tomatoes, peeled, seeded, and chopped**
Juice of 1 lime
1 **tablespoon tequila**

Yield: 6 servings
Color: Gold

Make a syrup by combining the water and sugar in a noncorrosive saucepan and bring to a boil. Simmer for 5 minutes and remove from the heat. Add the peppers and steep in the syrup for 20 minutes. Meanwhile, puree the mango, papaya, cantaloupe, yellow pepper, and saffron in a food processor or blender until smooth. Puree the yellow tomatoes and strain through a fine sieve. Remove the serrano peppers from the syrup and discard. Combine the syrup, lime juice, and tequila with the pureed ingredients. Freeze according to one of the methods in chapter 1.

4

SPIRITED SORBETS

Liqueurs and brandies have been used in supporting roles in some of the other ices in this book. Now they come to the forefront. You'll find some exciting recipes that explore the flavor possibilities of liqueurs, brandies, wine, and champagne.

What types of wine or liquors make the best sorbets? Well, if you can't drink it, don't cook with it. The best place for a wine that has been opened for a week is down your sink. The same holds true for the half-full bottles of brandies and cognacs that have been sitting on the bar cart for a couple of years. The alcohol will still be present, but its flavor will have diminished.

When it comes to cooking with spirits of any type, buy only what you need or think you'll be able to use over a reasonable period of time. It can be very expensive to buy a bottle of Chartreuse (or good cognac) for a recipe that calls for only a couple of tablespoons. So stock up on miniatures if they're available at your liquor store. And don't go to the extreme of using only the best that money can buy. Be realistic. There's a far better use for a bottle of Dom Perignon champagne than adding it to a fruit puree and freezing it. Nonetheless, good quality liqueurs and spirits are important in ice making, so choose according to your means.

When using wines in ice making, certain types work better than others. Some of the world's finest wines are a balance of subtle nuances. Some of those subtle characteristics will be lost when you mix the wine with sugar and citrus and then freeze it. Full-bodied red wines, such as Chateauneuf du Pape, Riojas, Chiantis, and Zinfandels, are hardy enough to be used in sorbets and granitas. Berry-flavored light reds, such as Beaujolais are also good choices. Bordeaux and some Cabernet Sauvignons are not.

White wines, such as some medium-priced domestic Chardonnays, spicy California Gewürtztraminers, and Rieslings are good bets. Paul Thomas Bartlett Pear Wine from Washington State makes a nice syrup substitute for pear ices. The domestic blush and rosé wines are chancy. The majority of these are blends that mix some decent quality grapes with some inferior ones. However, if you know the wine and like it — use it. Fortified wines, such as sherries, ports, and vermouths also make good bases for ices. And you really can't miss with decent champagne and sparklers.

You can really be creative with the wide range of brandies and cordials available. To get a good working flavor in your sorbet, you don't need a lot. When it comes to these liqueurs, less is more. The sweet liqueurs should not overpower the sorbet in either texture or flavor.

Since alcohol, like sugar syrup, lowers the freezing temperature, the proof of certain liqueurs has to be reduced or the sorbet will never freeze properly. The higher the proof — the lower the freezing point. For example, it takes longer to freeze a cup of cognac than it does to freeze a cup of wine. Cognac is 80 proof or 40 percent alcohol, where most wines contain around 10 to 14 percent alcohol. Too high a proof, or too much alcohol in relation to the other ingredients, can make your sorbet runny. You will be able to freeze the mixture initially, but when you try to serve it, you may find that it liquefies faster at room temperature than some of the fruit ices. And you may end up with some wonderful tasting puddles instead of a sorbet. Here's a way to handle some of the various spirits in ice making.

The best way to reduce the quantity of alcohol present is by flaming it. This applies to cordials, brandies, and distilled spirits (tequila, vodka, etc.). Simply bring the liquor to a simmer in a heavy noncorrosive saucepan (have a lid handy) and ignite the liquor with a match. Caution: High proof liquors (gin, vodka, etc.) will burn with a taller blue flame than a cordial, such as a fruit brandy, so keep the lid nearby to cover flare-ups. Higher proof liquors will also burn longer (and reduce more), so a careful eye is necessary to make sure your alcoholic flavors do not evaporate. When the alcohol burns off, you'll have a syrup essence that can be added to a sorbet or granita. Wines, champagnes, and fortified wines, such as sherries and vermouth, won't ignite.

Martini glasses, brandy snifters, and champagne saucers all make festive serving containers for spirited sorbets. White wine glasses (balloon goblets) also add to your presentation.

Guinness-Lime Sorbet

Here's a sorbet that can stand up to most robust stews and soups, and even gumbos. Guests will be besides themselves trying to pinpoint the flavor of stout and are delightfully surprised when you tell them.

1½ cups water
¾ cup sugar
1½ cups Guinness Stout
¼ cup fresh lime juice
Grated peel of 1 lime (1 teaspoon)
Lime twists to garnish

Yield: 6 servings
Color: Desert tan

Make a syrup by combining the water and sugar in a noncorrosive saucepan and bring to a boil. Simmer for 5 minutes. Remove from heat and cool. Combine the syrup, stout, lime juice, and peel. Freeze according to one of the methods in chapter 1.

To serve, scoop the sorbet into individual brandy snifters and garnish with lime twists.

Variation

Black Velvet Sorbet. Replace the sugar and water with 2 cups champagne (do not cook); replace the lime juice and peel with equal amounts of lemon juice and peel. Proceed with the recipe as above.

Grapefruit-Vermouth Sorbet

This classic ice from Chef Jean Banchet of La Francais in Wheeling, Illinois, will re-awaken and sharpen your taste buds. It does this without being too assertive and won't detract from the rest of your meal. Easy to prepare, this ice is great for formal sit-downs and makes a nice bridge between white and red wines.

4½ cups fresh grapefruit juice
10 tablespoons confectioners' sugar
½ cup good quality dry vermouth

Yield: 6 to 8 servings
Color: White

Combine the grapefruit juice, sugar, and vermouth. Freeze according to one of the methods in chapter 1. To serve, scoop the sorbet into individual champagne saucers and serve.

Champagne Sorbet

One of the easiest and most sophisticated ices one can make is this champagne sorbet. For a presentation that's as elegant as the sorbet, sauce a dessert plate with Raspberry Sauce (page 164) and top with 2 oval scoops of the sorbet (made with 2 large soup spoons). Garnish with sprigs of rosemary. During the spring and summer, you can also garnish this ice with sliced fresh strawberries or whole raspberries.

⅔ **cup water**
⅔ **cup sugar**
1 bottle (750 ml) dry pink or rosé champagne
Juice of ½ lemon
1 tablespoon fresh orange juice
1 egg white, beaten until stiff

Yield: 8 servings
Color: Pink

Make a syrup by combining the water and sugar in a noncorrosive saucepan and bring to a boil. Simmer for 5 minutes. Cool. Combine the syrup, champagne, and lemon and orange juices. Freeze according to one of the methods in chapter 1.

When the ice has frozen to a soft, slushy consistency, fold in the beaten egg white with a rubber spatula. Continue the freezing process until the ice is no longer slushy and has a firm texture. Serve in individual wine goblets.

Variation

Sauternes Sorbet. Substitute 1 bottle (750 ml) sauternes for the champagne, and reduce the sugar to ¼ cup. Proceed with the recipe as above.

Cantaloupe Champagne Sorbet

Winemaker Lee Miller of Chaddsford Winery in Brandywine, Pennsylvania, is the creator of this lovely light sorbet. Serve this ice in goblets with thin, crisp wafers and a sprig of mint. Chaddsford Sparkling Blush is excellent in this sorbet, but any champagne will do.

1 ripe cantaloupe
⅓ cup confectioners' sugar
1 cup champagne
Mint sprigs to garnish

Yield: 6 servings
Color: Light orange

Scoop out the fruit from the cantaloupe and place in a colander over a bowl to drain off the juice. Reserve the juice. Combine the cantaloupe pieces with the sugar and champagne in a noncorrosive saucepan. Bring to a boil. Simmer for 5 minutes. Remove from the heat and cool. Puree the mixture with the reserved cantaloupe juice in a food processor or blender. Freeze according to one of the methods in chapter 1. Serve garnished with mint.

Grapefruit Mimosa Sorbet

Grapefruit replaces the orange in this tart pink sorbet. You can serve this ice over fresh grapefruit slices in a large wine goblet for brunch, or you can wait until dinner and serve it as palate cleanser after a heavy salad or first course.

2½ cups champagne
¼ cup confectioners' sugar
1 cup fresh grapefruit juice (pink is recommended)
½ cup fresh lemon juice

Yield: 6 servings
Color: Pink

Combine the champagne, sugar, and grapefruit and lemon juices. Freeze according to one of the methods in chapter 1.

Variation

Mimosa Sorbet. Substitute fresh orange juice for the grapefruit juice and proceed with the recipe as above.

Sherry Sorbet

This sorbet is a good match for tapas and other highly seasoned appetizers. The citrus juices cut some of the sweetness of the sherry and enable you to serve this ice between courses. (Use sherry that is freshly opened; sherry that has been opened for a long period of time has a touch of bitterness. And do not use cooking sherry. Serve this sorbet in hazelnut Tulip Cups (page 168) or large cordial glasses.

2½ cups water
1 cup sugar
1 cup Amontillado sherry
½ cup fresh orange juice
¼ cup fresh lemon juice

Yield: 6 servings
Color: Tan

Make a syrup by combining the water and sugar in a noncorrosive saucepan and bring it to a boil. Simmer for 5 minutes. Remove from the heat and cool. Combine the syrup, sherry, and orange and lemon juices. Freeze according to one of the methods in chapter 1.

Nectarine-Rosé Sorbet

This sorbet has a wonderfully fragrant taste. It's a great palate cleanser that can follow a light soup. If possible, use a bottle of rosé from the Rhone Valley; if not, any good quality California blush Cabernet or blush Zinfandel can work as a substitute.

1 large lemon
2 cups rosé wine
½ cup sugar
8 to 9 fresh nectarines (1½ to 2 pounds)
Sliced nectarines to garnish

Yield: 6 servings
Color: Light peach

Peel the lemon and julienne the peel. Combine the wine with the lemon peel and sugar in a noncorrosive saucepan and bring to a boil. Add the nectarines, reduce the heat, and simmer for 45 to 50 minutes. Strain the liquid and reserve. Puree the solids with ¼ cup of the poaching liquid in a food processor or blender, then strain through a fine sieve. Combine with the remaining cooking liquid and cool. Freeze according to one of the methods in chapter 1.

To serve, form the sorbet into oval scoops and garnish with sliced nectarines.

Prune Plum Sorbet

The first thing you notice about this ice is it's wonderful hint of Madeira, though no Madeira is used. What makes the taste particularly interesting is the poaching spices that complement the plums. This dessert sorbet goes well with southern Italian cooking.

2 pounds fresh prune plums, pitted and chopped
2 cups ruby port
½ cup sugar
Pinch cardamom
1 cinnamon stick
3 cloves
1 strip lemon peel
Juice of 1 lemon

Yield: 6 servings
Color: Light purple

Combine the plums with the port, sugar, and cardamom in a noncorrosive saucepan. Wrap the cinnamon stick, cloves, and lemon peel in a damp cheesecloth and add to the plum mixture. Bring to a boil. Simmer for 30 to 40 minutes, until the plums are soft and tender. Remove the cheesecloth, strain the mixture, and reserve the liquid. Puree the solids with ¼ cup of the reserved liquid in a food processor or blender, then strain through a fine sieve. Combine the puree with the rest of the reserved liquid and cool. Combine with the lemon juice. Freeze according to one of the methods in chapter 1.

Marsala Sorbet

The addition of golden raisins to the Marsala brings an intense depth of flavor to this dessert sorbet. You'll find hints of dessert wines, as well as the taste of Marsala in this ice. By the way, no additional sugar is needed in this recipe because of the sugar content of the raisins.

2 cups Marsala
⅔ cup golden raisins
Peel of 1 lemon (white pith removed)
1½ cups water
¼ cup fresh lemon juice

Yield: 6 servings
Color: Tan

Combine the Marsala, raisins, and lemon peel in a heavy-bottom noncorrosive saucepan and bring to a boil. Simmer uncovered for 1 hour. In the end, the mixture should yield less than 2 cups. Remove from the heat and cool. Puree with ½ cup of the water in a food processor or blender. Strain through a fine sieve. Combine the raisin/Marsala mixture, the remaining 1 cup water, and lemon juice. Freeze according to one of the methods in chapter 1.

Variation

Madeira Sorbet. Substitute 2 cups Madeira for the Marsala and ⅔ cup dried black currants for the raisins. Proceed with the recipe as above.

Coconut Galliano Sorbet

The combination of coconut and the vanilla flavor of Galliano is positively habit forming. The sorbet also has a nice burst of tartness from the lime. This easy dessert sorbet is one that can be made a few days ahead and still hold it's flavor.

½ cup Galliano
1¾ cups water
1 (15-ounce) can coconut cream
½ cup fresh lime juice

Yield: 6 servings
Color: Ivory

In a noncorrosive saucepan, simmer the Galliano, ignite with a match to flame, and reduce by about one third. Remove from the heat and cool. Combine the water and coconut cream. Add the Galliano and lime juice. Freeze according to one of the methods in chapter 1.

Mango Daiquiri Sorbet

A daiquiri of any flavor makes a great summer sorbet. But using a standard daiquiri formula will produce a very watery ice. So you have to adjust the mixture in order to properly freeze and form it into a sorbet. The following recipe should do the trick.

⅔ **cup water**
⅓ **cup sugar**
1 cup rum
2 cups mango puree
⅔ **cup fresh lime juice**

Yield: 6 servings
Color: Yellow

Make a syrup by combining the water and sugar in a noncorrosive saucepan and bring to a boil. Simmer for 5 minutes. Remove from the heat and cool.

In a noncorrosive saucepan, bring the rum to a simmer, ignite with a match, and flame to reduce the rum by half. Then remove from the heat and cool. Combine the syrup, rum, mango puree, and lime juice. Freeze according to one of the methods in chapter 1.

Variation

Strawberry Daiquiri Sorbet. Substitute 2 cups pureed strawberries for the mango and proceed with the recipe as above.

Calvados Sorbet

Here is a basic spirited sorbet with several variations to give just a sample of the range of flavors that are to be found in cordials and liqueurs. Serve these sorbets in large brandy snifters.

2 cups water
1 cup sugar
1-inch piece cinnamon stick
¾ cup calvados
1 cup apple cider
¼ cup fresh lemon juice

Yield: 6 servings
Color: Tan

Make a syrup by combining the water, sugar, and cinnamon stick in a noncorrosive saucepan and bring to a boil. Simmer for 5 minutes. Remove from the heat and cool. Remove the cinnamon stick from the syrup and discard.

In a noncorrosive saucepan, bring the calvados to a simmer, ignite with a match, and flame to reduce the calvados by one-half. Then remove from the heat and cool. Combine the syrup, calvados, cider, and the lemon juice. Freeze according to one of the methods in chapter 1.

Variation

Rum Sorbet. Substitute dark rum for the calvados, ⅔ cup fresh orange juice and ⅓ cup dry white wine for the apple cider, and lime juice for the lemon juice. Proceed with the recipe as above.

Orange Liqueur Sorbet. Substitute julienned orange peel for the cinnamon; Cointreau (or Grand Marnier) for the calvados; and 1 cup orange juice for the apple cider. Proceed with the recipe as above.

Cognac/Brandy Sorbet. Substitute ¾ cup cognac or brandy for the calvados, and ⅔ cup fresh orange juice and ⅓ cup dry white wine for the apple cider. Proceed with the recipe as above.

Marc/Grappa Sorbet. Substitute ¾ cup marc or grappa for the calvados, ½ cup unsweetened white grape juice and ½ cup dry Italian white wine for the apple cider. *Note*: if you are using marc, try to use a similar wine; substitute unsweetened Ribier grape juice if the marc is from a red wine. Proceed with the recipe as above.

Poire William Sorbet

This intensely flavored pear sorbet is from Jon Jividen, executive chef of the Philadelphia/Washington, D.C.-based Ridgewell's (caterer for the White House). For a truly elegant dessert, try serving this ice over a fan of poached pears.

⅔ **cup water**
⅔ **cup sugar**
3 pounds fresh ripe pears
6 tablespoons fresh lemon juice
½ **cup Poire William or pear schnapps**

Yield: 6 servings
Color: Light pinkish tan

Make a syrup by combining the water and sugar in a noncorrosive saucepan and bring to a boil. Simmer for 5 minutes. Remove from the heat and cool.

Puree the pears in a food processor or blender (if pears are not ripe and soft, slice and simmer the pears in the syrup mixture until soft enough to puree). Strain the pear puree through a fine sieve and add the sugar syrup, lemon juice, and Poire William. Freeze according to one of the methods in chapter 1.

Midori Sorbet

This neon green sorbet tastes as cool as it looks. The tart lime juice offsets the sweetness of the Midori (melon liqueur) and rum and brings this ice into balance. The ripe honeydew brings additional color and a refreshing coolness to the other flavors. This sorbet could be served with sushi or any cold seafood appetizers.

⅔ **cup Midori or other melon liqueur**
⅓ **cup white rum**
3 cups diced honeydew melon
⅓ **cup fresh lime juice**
Melon balls and fresh sprigs of mint to garnish

Yield: 6 servings
Color: Bright green

In a noncorrosive saucepan, combine the Midori and rum. Bring to a low simmer. Then ignite with a match and flame to reduce the mixture by about one-third (you should have ½ to ⅔ cup). Remove from the heat and cool.

Puree the honeydew in a blender or food processor. Combine the Midori/rum mixture, the honeydew puree, and the lime juice. Freeze according to one of the methods in chapter 1.

Garnish with melon balls and fresh sprigs of mint.

Gin Sorbet

In some European restaurants, a small glass of gin will sometimes arrive between courses as a palate cleanser. Gin is one of the best distilled spirits for that particular purpose. This sorbet extends that tradition in a refreshing way.

1½ cups water
½ cup sugar
6 to 8 whole juniper berries (available in the spice department of most supermarkets)
¾ cup gin
¼ cup fresh lime juice
½ cup tonic water

Yield: 6 servings
Color: White

Make a syrup by combining the water, sugar, and juniper berries in a noncorrosive saucepan and bring to a boil. Simmer for 5 minutes. Remove from the heat, discard the juniper berries, and cool.

Pour the gin into a noncorrosive saucepan, simmer on low; then ignite with a match, and flame to reduce the gin by one-half. Combine the syrup, reduced gin, lime juice, and tonic water. Freeze according to one of the methods in chapter 1. Serve in large cordial glasses.

Banana Rum Sorbet

The taste of that traditional New Orleans dessert, Bananas Foster, is captured in this sorbet — a splendid capping to an evening of Cajun-Creole cooking.

4 to 5 ripe bananas
¼ teaspoon cinnamon
¼ cup brown sugar
¼ cup dark rum (preferably Meyer's)
1 cup water
⅓ cup granulated sugar
Juice of 2 limes (about ¼ cup)

Yield: 6 servings
Color: Tan

Peel and slice the bananas in half lengthwise and place them flat side up in a heat-resistant glass or porcelain baking dish. Sprinkle the cinnamon and brown sugar over the bananas. Pour the rum over the bananas and brown under a broiler for about 5 minutes. Remove the bananas and reserve. Pour the juices from the baking dish into a small noncorrosive saucepan, bring to a simmer, ignite the liquid with a match, and reduce the volume by one-third. Add the water and sugar to the reduced liquid and bring to a boil. Simmer for 5 minutes. Remove from the heat and cool.

Combine the bananas and syrup mixture in a food processor or blender and puree. Add the lime juice. Freeze according to one of the methods in chapter 1.

Margarita-Jalapeño Sorbet

This sorbet starts off gently and you find yourself savoring the tart lime and tequila. But then, at the back of your mouth, the jalapeño kicks in and throws your whole sense of taste into a tailspin. How can something this spicy be this cool?

1 cup water
½ cup sugar
2 fresh jalapeño peppers, halved and seeded
½ cup tequila
¼ cup fresh lime juice
¼ cup Triple Sec or any other orange liqueur
Lime wedges to garnish (optional)

Yield: 6 servings
Color: White

Make a syrup by combining the water and sugar in a noncorrosive saucepan. Bring to a boil and then reduce the heat to allow the mixture to simmer. Add the peppers to the saucepan and steep in the mixture for 10 to 15 minutes. Remove the jalapeños with a slotted spoon and discard. Strain the mixture and cool. Combine the tequila, lime juice, and Triple Sec with the cooled syrup. Freeze according to one of the methods in chapter 1. Serve the sorbet in frosted martini glasses and garnish with lime wedges.

Tequila Lime Sorbet

Served as a refreshing dessert at the Border Grill in Los Angeles by Co-Chefs Mary Sue Milliken and Susan Feniger, this sorbet is elegant enough to find its way into a formal dinner as tart palate cleanser.

For a nice presentation, dip the rims of individual champagne saucers in lime juice, then sugar, and chill. Add the sorbet and serve with a slice of lime.

3½ cups water
1½ cups sugar
¾ cup quality tequila (Cuervo Gold is recommended)
1¼ cups fresh lime juice
1 egg white, beaten until stiff

Yield: 8 servings
Color: Greenish white

Make a syrup by combining the water and sugar in a noncorrosive saucepan and bring to a boil. Simmer for 5 minutes. Remove from the heat and cool.

Pour the tequila into a noncorrosive saucepan, ignite with a match, and flame to reduce the volume by one-third. Remove the tequila from the heat and cool.

Combine the syrup mixture, tequila, and lime juice. Freeze according to one of the methods in chapter 1.

When the ice has frozen to a soft, slushy consistency, fold in the beaten egg white with a rubber spatula. Continue the freezing process until the ice is no longer slushy and has a firm texture.

Vodka Lemon Sorbet

Icy cold vodka and lemon: what a combination! You can serve this sorbet with a light summer dinner or a multi-course New Year's Eve buffet.

¾ cup vodka (Stolichnaya is
   recommended)
3 cups water
1½ cups sugar
1¼ cups fresh lemon juice
1 egg white, beaten until stiff
Lemon peel spirals to garnish

Yield: 6 servings
Color: White

Heat the vodka in a noncorrosive heavy-bottom saucepan, ignite with a match, and flame to reduce the vodka by one-third. Set aside.

Make a syrup by combining the water and sugar in a noncorrosive saucepan and bring to a boil. Simmer for 5 minutes. Remove from the heat and cool. Combine the reduced vodka, sugar syrup, and lemon juice. Freeze according to one of the methods in chapter 1.

When the ice has frozen to a soft, slushy consistency, fold in the beaten egg white with a rubber spatula. Continue the freezing process until the ice is no longer slushy and has a firm texture. Serve in champagne saucers garnished with lemon spirals.

5
PANTRY SORBETS

As soon as there's a nip in the fall air, many of us start to get ambitious in the kitchen. But when it comes to cooking, nature does not play fair. During the summer, with the abundance of fresh fruit and vegetables, all we feel like doing is grilling—anything that has ever moved, flown, grown, or swum. But come mid-winter, when there is time to go the whole seven courses, we're scrambling for fresh ingredients. When it comes to sorbets, the trick, of course, is to stock up the freezer with frozen fruit purees. But that will only get us so far. What we need to find are alternatives to fresh ingredients.

Pantry Sorbets are ices that can be created with ingredients that are found around most kitchens: teas, dried and canned fruit, and even chocolate. When fondues go plop and carrot cakes flop, these sorbets can help you keep your cool.

Let's start with some obvious sources of ingredients—like the tin can. In it you can find everything from kumquats to litchis.

Oriental grocery stores have some of the largest selections of canned exotic fruit that you'll ever find. Not only will you find fruit, but that fruit will be packed in its own syrup, which can be used in a sorbet.

If you're the type that puts up canned fruit in the summer and fall, then you really have it made. Simply strain the fruit syrup and add additional sugar syrup if necessary to make 1 full cup. Then follow one of the corresponding recipes in the Fruit Sorbets chapter, using canned fruit instead of fresh. And frozen fruit will work just as well. If you happen to have a 10-ounce package of frozen raspberries or strawberries on hand, puree the berries and strain, add the juice of ½ lemon and a tablespoon of raspberry liqueur (you won't need to add a sugar syrup since most frozen fruits are packed in a light syrup), follow one of the methods in chapter 1, and you've got yourself a sorbet.

Fruit jams and jellies when heated will

yield a consistent syrup that you may want to make into a sorbet. Simply dilute the melted jam with an equal amount of water and freeze according to one of the methods in chapter 1 for an ice with a highly intense fruit flavor. Gourmet jams, such as jalapeño, mint, or ginger, as well as liqueured fruit jellies and preserves, will also make some phenomenal syrup bases to add to fresh fruit purees to make some very exciting ices.

Also from your pantry are dried herbs and spices. Adding either crystallized ginger, a cinnamon stick, or a vanilla bean while simmering your sugar syrup will enhance certain recipes. Anise seeds will give a slight licorice flavor and cardamom seeds can create a sorbet with hints of the exotic East.

There is a tendency to feel that prepackaged ingredients are inferior to fresh ones. It simply depends on the context of the meal and how creatively the ingredients are used. Freshness won't guarantee a great sorbet — or even a great meal for that matter.

Red Zinger Sorbet

This bright red palate cleanser is from Jimmy Schmidt, chef at the Rattlesnake Club in Denver, Colorado. This Red Zinger Sorbet is nice to serve after a smoked chicken or duck breast salad.

2½ cups water
⅔ cup sugar
6 Red Zinger tea bags or 2 heaping
 tablespoons loose Red Zinger tea
½ lemon, juiced

Yield: 6 servings
Color: Red

In a noncorrosive saucepan, combine the water and the sugar and bring to a boil. Remove from the heat, add the tea, and steep until the flavor is well developed, about 15 minutes. Remove the tea bags or strain the tea and cool. Combine the tea with the lemon juice. Freeze according to one of the methods in chapter 1.

Orange Spice Sorbet

This sorbet starts off by behaving like an orange ice but finishes with a nice spicy afterglow. Serve with a garnish of litchi nuts after a Thai or Chinese main dish.

3 cups water
1 cup sugar
3 heaping tablespoons orange spice tea
    leaves
½ cup fresh orange juice
¼ cup fresh lemon juice
Pinch cumin

Yield: 6 servings
Color: Ivory

Make a syrup by combining the water and sugar in a noncorrosive saucepan and bring to a boil. Simmer for 5 minutes. Remove from the heat, add the tea, and steep for 15 to 20 minutes. Strain the syrup and combine with the orange and lemon juices and cumin. Freeze according to one of the methods in chapter 1.

Lemon Grass Sorbet

Dried lemon grass, available in Oriental grocery stores, is an herb that gives zing to Thai cuisine. It will last forever in the produce drawer of your refrigerator. Dried lemon grass tea can be used in this recipe as well. This sorbet has a nice touch of lemon-lime heat. Serve it to complement a beef or chicken saté with peanut sauce, or any other Thai dish.

1 cup water
½ cup sugar
1 stalk dried lemon grass or 2
    tablespoons lemon grass tea
¼ cup fresh lemon juice
Grated peel of 1 lemon

Yield: 6 servings
Color: White

Make a syrup by combining the water and sugar in a noncorrosive saucepan. Bring to a boil and simmer. Coarsely chop the lemon grass, add to the syrup, and simmer for 20 to 25 minutes. Remove from the heat and cool. Strain the mixture, discard the lemon grass, and combine with the lemon juice and peel. Freeze according to one of the methods in chapter 1.

Saffron Sorbet

The fragrance of this bright yellow sorbet fills the room when it's served. The traditional combination of saffron and rose water is used throughout the Middle East in desserts and cold drinks. Enjoy one spoonful of this ice and you'll see why the tradition has lasted as long as it has! This sorbet is also savory enough to follow first-course seafood dishes.

Scant ¼ teaspoon saffron threads
3 cups water
1½ cups sugar
½ cup fresh orange juice
¼ cup fresh lemon juice
1 tablespoon rose water

Yield: 6 servings
Color: Sunshine yellow

Make a syrup by crushing the saffron and combining it with the water and sugar in a noncorrosive saucepan. Bring to a boil. Simmer for 10 to 15 minutes. Remove from the heat, cool to room temperature, and then strain. Combine the saffron mixture, orange and lemon juices, and rose water. Freeze according to one of the methods in chapter 1. Form the sorbet with an ice cream scoop and serve in individual martini glasses.

White Chocolate-Chocolate Chip Sorbet

A chocolate dessert made without eggs and heavy cream? This dessert actually tastes richer than it is. The crème de cassis gives the ice added flavor. This frozen treat looks great served in marbled Chocolate Shells (page 167) and garnished with fresh raspberries or strawberries and mint.

2½ cups water

⅓ cup sugar

½ vanilla bean, split, or ½ teaspoon pure vanilla extract

6 ounces good quality white chocolate, finely chopped

1 teaspoon crème de cassis (black currant liqueur)

¼ cup good quality semi-sweet chocolate, chopped into small pieces

Yield: 6 servings
Color: White with brown dots

Make a syrup by combining the water, sugar, and vanilla bean (do not add vanilla extract at this time) in a noncorrosive saucepan and bring to a boil. Simmer for 5 minutes. Transfer the syrup to the top of a double boiler set over hot water and slowly stir in the white chocolate until it dissolves and is no longer grainy. *Note*: Do not let mixture boil or the chocolate will separate. Remove the vanilla bean with a slotted spoon. Remove the white chocolate mixture from the heat and cool. Combine the white chocolate mixture with the crème de cassis. Add the vanilla extract (if you are not using a vanilla bean). Freeze according to one of the methods in chapter 1.

When the ice has frozen to a soft, slushy consistency, fold in the semi-sweet chocolate with a rubber spatula. Continue the freezing process until the ice is no longer slushy and has a firm texture.

Variations

White Chocolate Mint Sorbet. Steep 1 tablespoon fresh mint in the syrup solution for about 10 minutes, remove, then add the white chocolate. Substitute 1 teaspoon crème de menthe for the crème de cassis. Proceed with the recipe as above.

Chocolate Sorbet with Raspberry Sauce. You can reverse the colors in this sorbet by substituting 6 ounces of quality semi-sweet chocolate for the white chocolate, 2 ounces white chocolate chopped into small pieces for the semi-sweet chocolate, and 1 teaspoon Grand Marnier for the cassis. Proceed with the sorbet recipe as above. To serve, sauce individual dessert plates with Raspberry Sauce (page 164). Form the sorbet into large oval scoops and arrange on serving plates.

Pumpkin Sorbet

This sorbet tastes like a light frozen pumpkin mousse. For a spectacular ending to an autumn dinner, serve this sorbet in Brandy Snap Baskets (page 169).

2 cups water
½ cup pure maple syrup
¼ cup brown sugar
1½ cups canned or cooked pumpkin (not pumpkin pie filling)
1 teaspoon cinnamon
½ teaspoon ground ginger
¼ teaspoon ground allspice
¼ teaspoon nutmeg
2 egg whites
2 tablespoons confectioners' sugar
1 tablespoon brandy

Yield: 6 servings
Color: Brown

Combine the water, maple syrup, and brown sugar in a noncorrosive saucepan and bring to a boil. Reduce the heat and simmer. Add the pumpkin, cinnamon, ginger, allspice, and nutmeg and simmer for 45 to 50 minutes. Remove from the heat and strain through a fine sieve. Cool and strain again. Freeze according to one of the methods in chapter 1.

Beat the egg whites until they form soft peaks. Add the confectioners' sugar and brandy, and beat again until the peaks are stiff and shiny. When the ice has frozen to a soft, slushy consistency, fold in the beaten egg whites with a rubber spatula. Continue the freezing process until the ice is no longer slushy and has a firm texture.

Dried Apricot Sorbet

You can create other sorbet flavors with dried fruit, such as pineapple or even papaya. And you can mix the flavors by adding different kinds of jams or preserves for contrast. Your creativity is only limited by what you have stocked in your pantry.

1 cup dried apricots
3 cups water
¼ cup fresh orange juice
½ cup apricot preserves
1 tablespoon apricot brandy (optional)

Yield: 6 servings
Color: Yellow

Combine the apricots and water in a noncorrosive saucepan and bring to a boil. Simmer for 45 minutes, or until the apricots soften and expand. Remove from the heat, strain out the apricots, and reserve the cooking liquid.

Combine the apricots and the orange juice and puree in a food processor or blender. Strain the apricot puree through a fine sieve and set aside.

Make a syrup by combining the cooking liquid and the apricot preserves in a noncorrosive saucepan, bring to a boil, then simmer until the preserves and sugar dissolves, about 5 minutes. Combine the apricot puree, syrup mixture, and brandy. Freeze according to one of the methods in chapter 1.

Litchi Sorbet

Fresh litchi nuts are difficult to find. And once you do find them, they can put up quite a fight while you're trying to prepare them. Canned litchi nuts work just as well. No need to keep this sorbet on reserve for Chinese food alone.

2 cups canned litchi nuts with syrup
½ cup water
1½ cups pink or rosé champagne
1 lime, juice and peel
Mango Sauce (page 164) (optional)

Yield: 6 servings
Color: Light pink

Drain the litchi nuts, reserve the syrup, and puree with the water in a food processor or blender. Combine the litchi puree, reserved syrup, champagne, and lime juice. Freeze according to one of the methods in chapter 1.

Sauce individual dessert plates with the Mango Sauce. Form the sorbet into oval scoops and place over the sauce. Garnish with strips of lime peel.

Variation

Peach Champagne Sorbet. Substitute 2 cups sliced canned peaches for the litchi nuts and 1 lemon for the lime. Add 1 tablespoon peach brandy or peach schnapps to the fruit puree. Proceed with the recipe as above.

Mango Chutney Sorbet

In an ice, chutneys deliver highly seasoned fruit flavor with a tremendous array of taste sensations. This Mango Chutney Sorbet is no exception. From the first spoonful, you get a taste of the sweet mangoes. Then the spices open up and the other flavors begin to unfold. Although serving chutney sorbets to accompany Indian cuisine is a good choice, this sorbet can work even better as part of a salad presentation.

1 (17-ounce) jar mango chutney or 2
  cups homemade chutney
1½ cups water
½ cup sugar
1 tablespoon fresh lime juice

Yield: 6 servings
Color: Orange

In a noncorrosive saucepan, combine the chutney with the water and sugar. Simmer until the chutney liquefies, 15 to 20 minutes. Remove from the heat and cool. Puree the chutney mixture in a food processor until smooth. Strain the mixture and add the lime juice. Freeze according to one of the methods in chapter 1.

Marmalade Sorbet

The deep, tangy taste of orange marmalade is captured in this ice. The better the quality of marmalade, the better the ice, so go for the English imports if you really want to savor what good Seville oranges have to offer.

2 cups orange marmalade
1 cup water
1 cup fresh orange juice
1 tablespoon julienned orange peel
¼ cup fresh lemon juice
1 tablespoon Amontillado sherry or other
   medium-dry sherry
Julienned orange peel to garnish

Yield: 6 servings
Color: Orange

Combine the marmalade, water, orange juice, and 1 tablespoon orange peel in a noncorrosive saucepan and simmer until the marmalade liquefies and the mixture becomes syrupy. Remove from the heat and cool. Combine the marmalade mixture with the lemon juice and sherry. Freeze according to one of the methods in chapter 1.

Garnish individual servings with julienned orange peel.

6
Pure Fruit Ices

Pure Fruit Ices are sorbets that are made without sugar syrups or liquors. Unsweetened fruit juices and natural fruit sugars (fructose) act as sugar (sucrose) syrup substitutes. Not only do these ices have a lower calorie count than traditional sorbets, but they are easier to make because there is no sugar syrup to prepare beforehand. There may be a slight difference in texture; that is, some of these ices may not be as smooth as a typical sorbet.

The best time to serve these ices is almost immediately after you make them. The fruit flavors will be at their peak, and the consistency of the ice will be just right. Because of the lower sugar content, some of these ices will freeze to a solid block if left in the freezer overnight. When that happens, you have a couple of options. You can remove the ice from your freezer and place it in the refrigerator for a couple of hours. Then pulse it in small batches in a blender or food processor to the desired consistency. Scoop the ice into chilled glasses or individual bowls and keep them in the freezer until you're ready to serve. They should stay in your freezer at this point for no longer than 30 minutes. Another option involves freezing the mixture in a glass or nonmetal container and requires a microwave oven. Remove the ice from your freezer, place it, covered, in a microwave oven, and heat at 100 percent power for 1½ minutes. Then serve.

For these recipes to work, it's absolutely essential to use fresh, ripe produce. Fruit that is underripe will lack flavor intensity. You can hasten the ripening process by sealing the fruit overnight in a plastic bag with a banana. The ethylene gas given off by the banana triggers the enzymes present in fruit to start the ripening process. If all of your produce doesn't ripen at the same pace, gently simmer the underripe fruit in either apple or pineapple juice for 10 to 15 minutes or until soft. Drain the mixture and allow the fruit to cool, then proceed with the rest of the recipe.

Sorbets contain fewer calories than ice cream, and these ices contain fewer still. For example, the Papaya Sorbet on page 56 contains about 685 calories. Dividing that up among 6 servings yields about 115 calories per portion, with the sugar syrup accounting for over half the calorie count. The Papaya-Passion Fruit Ice on page 141 has about 425 calories, yielding about 70 calories per serving. So you can see that the chief advantage of the following recipes is their lower calorie count.

Although these recipes contain neither granulated sugar nor other sweeteners, they are not sugar free. The sucrose in granulated sugar is replaced by fructose, a natural sugar present in fruit. When considering whether or not to serve these ices to guests with dietary restrictions, check with your guests first.

Since you will be using fresh fruit, you can garnish these ices with the actual fruit used in the recipe. The results will be spectacular!

Apple-Currant Ice

By using Granny Smith apples, this sorbet becomes a nice tart palate cleanser. The black currants give the ice its sweetness and color. You'll be able to serve this sorbet to follow a salad course or cold appetizers.

2 cups fresh black currants
1 cup unsweetened apple juice
2 cups peeled and chopped Granny Smith apples
¼ cup fresh lemon juice
1 egg white, beaten until stiff
Additional currants and fresh mint sprigs to garnish

Yield: 6 servings
Color: Deep red

Remove the stems from the currants and combine with the apple juice in a noncorrosive saucepan. Simmer for 45 to 50 minutes. Add the chopped apples and simmer until the apple chunks are soft, about 30 minutes. Strain and reserve the liquid. Puree the solids in a food processor with ½ cup of the liquid. Then strain through a fine sieve. Combine the liquid, fruit puree, and lemon juice. Freeze according to one of the methods in chapter 1.

When the ice has frozen to a soft, slushy consistency, fold in the beaten egg white with a rubber spatula. Continue the freezing process until the ice is no longer slushy and has a firm texture. Serve in individual dessert bowls and garnish with currants and fresh mint.

Cranberry Apple Ice

This sorbet is tart enough to serve with one-dish soups or stews. It also works nicely with spicy chili. The cranberries provide the color and tartness while the apples gently sweeten. The combination of cinnamon and cardamom gives this ice somewhat of a Middle Eastern flavor.

1 (12-ounce) package fresh or frozen cranberries
½ cup fresh orange juice
2 Granny Smith apples, chopped
½ cup apple juice or cider
4 whole cardamom pods
1 cinnamon stick

Yield: 6 servings
Color: Red

Combine the cranberries and orange juice in a noncorrosive saucepan and simmer until the cranberries burst from their skins. Cool the mixture and puree in a food processor or blender. Strain through a fine sieve and cool in the refrigerator.

While the cranberries simmer, combine the apples with the apple juice, cardamom, and cinnamon in a noncorrosive saucepan. Simmer for 20 minutes. Discard the cardamom pods and cinnamon stick and puree the apple mixture in a food processor. Strain through a fine sieve, then cool. Combine the cranberry and apple purees. Freeze according to one of the methods in chapter 1.

Blueberry Kiwi Ice

With this ice the flavors change with each spoonful. First comes the blueberries, and when you're almost convinced that you are eating a blueberry sorbet, the flavor of the kiwis kicks in with a little bit of vanilla on the back end.

1 cup fresh blueberries
1 cup unsweetened apple juice
½ vanilla bean, split
8 ripe kiwi fruit
¼ cup fresh lemon juice

Yield: 6 servings
Color: Dark blue

Combine the blueberries, apple juice, and vanilla bean in a noncorrosive pot. Simmer until the blueberries burst. Remove from the heat and cool. When the blueberry mixture has cooled to room temperature, discard the vanilla bean, and puree the mixture in a food processor or blender. Then strain through a fine sieve and refrigerate for 1 hour.

Peel the kiwis and puree in a food mill (you should have about 2 cups). Combine the blueberry and the kiwi mixtures. Freeze according to one of the methods in chapter 1.

Strawberry-Watermelon Ice

This summer cooler is perfect by itself. It is more of a thirst quencher than a palate cleanser. Eating it is one of the best ways of dealing with the dog days of August.

1 ripe banana
1 pint strawberries
2 cups chopped watermelon
½ cup fresh orange juice
¼ cup fresh lemon juice
Mint leaves to garnish

Yield: 6 servings
Color: Red

Puree the banana, strawberries, and watermelon in a food processor or blender until the mixture is smooth. Strain through a fine sieve and combine with the orange and lemon juices. Freeze according to one of the methods in chapter 1. Garnish each serving with mint leaves.

Banana-Strawberry Ice

The banana in this easy-to-make sorbet makes it appear almost as creamy as ice cream. This is a nice light dessert sorbet to serve throughout strawberry season.

1 pint fresh strawberries
1 ripe banana
1 cup unsweetened pineapple juice
½ cup fresh orange juice

Yield: 6 servings
Color: Pink

Halve 6 strawberries and reserve for the garnish. Puree the remaining strawberries with the banana in a food processor. Then combine the puree with the pineapple and orange juices. Freeze according to one of the methods in chapter 1. Garnish each serving with 2 strawberry halves.

Mango Raspberry Ice

The tart raspberry is gently sweetened by the ripe mango in this ice. For a nice dessert presentation, combine with the Blueberry Kiwi Ice (page 126) and the Pineapple Citrus Ice (page 134). Garnish with sliced kiwis and mangoes, lime zest, and fresh blueberries and raspberries.

½ **pint fresh raspberries**
2 **cups chopped mango (about 2 small or**
   1 large yellow-skinned mango)
½ **cup unsweetened pineapple juice**
   (fresh or bottled)
½ **cup fresh orange juice**
Grated peel of 1 orange
Juice of ½ lemon
Juice of 1 lime

Yield: 6 servings
Color: Maroon

Puree the raspberries in a food processor or blender and strain through a fine sieve. Puree the mangoes in a food processor or blender and combine with the raspberry puree, pineapple juice, orange juice and peel, and lemon and lime juices. Freeze according to one of the methods in chapter 1.

Raspberry-Peach Ice

If you're lucky enough to find white peaches during the summer, this sorbet will really sparkle. Arrange small oval scoops of this sorbet with Blueberry Kiwi Ice (page 126) and Papaya-Passion Fruit Ice (page 141) and separate each sorbet with slices of fresh papaya, peach, and kiwi. For additional color, garnish with fresh raspberries and blueberries.

1 cup fresh raspberries
3 ripe peaches, peeled
½ cup fresh pineapple juice
½ cup fresh orange juice
1 egg white, beaten until stiff

Yield: 6 servings
Color: Pink-orange

Puree the raspberries in a food processor or blender and strain through a fine sieve. Puree the peaches with the pineapple and orange juices in a food processor or blender. Combine the raspberry and peach purees. Freeze according to one of the methods in chapter 1.

When the ice has frozen to a soft, slushy consistency, fold in the beaten egg white with a rubber spatula. Continue the freezing process until the ice is no longer slushy and has a firm texture.

Grape-Lime Ice

This is a sorbet with a bit of tang. It can be served after a fish course. You can easily substitute dark grapes, such as Concord or Ribier, or red grape juice for the green grape juice to produce a sorbet of an entirely different character.

1½ **cups unsweetened green (white) grape**
    juice
¼ **cup fresh lime juice**
½ **cup mineral water**
1 **egg white, beaten until stiff**
1 **dozen fresh grapes and sprigs of mint**
    for garnish

Yield: 6 servings
Color: White

Combine the grape juice, lime juice, and mineral water. Freeze according to one of the methods in chapter 1.

When the ice has frozen to a soft, slushy consistency, fold in the beaten egg white with a rubber spatula. Continue the freezing process until the ice is no longer slushy and has a firm texture.

Serve this sorbet in champagne flutes and garnish each serving with 2 grapes and sprigs of mint.

Cucumber Melon Ice

The mint and cucumber provide the cool, refreshing feeling in the ice, while the citrus and ginger provide the tang. This ice could be served as a first course salad sorbet over grapefruit slices and greens.

½ **honeydew melon**
1 **medium-size cucumber, peeled, seeded, and chopped into 1-inch pieces**
2 **tablespoons finely chopped fresh mint**
1 **tablespoon minced fresh ginger root**
1 **cup fresh grapefruit juice**
¼ **cup fresh lime juice**

Yield: 6 servings
Color: Green

In a food processor or blender, puree the melon with the cucumber and measure out 2 cups of puree. Then puree the mint and ginger with the melon/cucumber puree in a food processor or blender. Combine the puree with the grapefruit and lime juices. Freeze according to one of the methods in chapter 1.

Bellini Ice

This ice is fashioned after the Italian drink, the Bellini, a peach and white wine sparkler. What we have in this recipe are the flavors of tart white grape juice with ripe sweet peaches. For a really nice summer dessert, place some fresh peach slices in a large wine goblet, top with the Bellini ice, and garnish with a kiwi slice.

2 to 3 fresh peaches, peeled
2 cups unsweetened white grape juice
1 cup lemon/lime seltzer
¼ cup fresh lime juice

Yield: 6 servings
Color: Peach

Puree the peaches in a food processor to yield about 1 cup. Combine the peach puree, grape juice, seltzer, and lime juice. Freeze according to one of the methods in chapter 1.

Pineapple Citrus Ice

The sweet fresh pineapple in this recipe provides a nice contrast to the tart grapefruit and lime juices. This ice makes a wonderful brunch sorbet you can serve all year-round.

3 to 4 cups fresh pineapple chunks
1 cup fresh orange juice
½ cup fresh grapefruit juice
¼ cup fresh lime juice
1 egg white, beaten until stiff

Yield: 6 servings
Color: Light yellow

Puree the pineapple with the orange juice in a food processor or blender. Strain the mixture through a fine sieve and combine with the grapefruit and lime juices. Freeze according to one of the methods in chapter 1.

When the ice has frozen to a soft, slushy consistency, fold in the beaten egg white with a rubber spatula. Continue the freezing process until the ice is no longer slushy and has a firm texture.

Ginger-Fig Ice

Your first spoonful of this ice will give you the impression that there are more ingredients at work than there actually are! You'll easily taste the ginger and figs, but when they start to interact, other flavors seem to emerge. Use ripe purple figs and, if you like, garnish with diced prosciutto.

1-inch square fresh ginger root, minced
1½ cups fresh orange juice
**2 cups fig puree (about 12 purple figs,
    peeled and pureed)**
Juice of ½ lemon

Yield: 6 servings
Color: Rust

Combine the ginger with ¾ cup of the orange juice in a noncorrosive saucepan. Simmer until the ginger softens, about 20 minutes. Combine the ginger/orange mixture, the remaining ¾ cup orange juice, the fig puree, and lemon juice. Freeze according to one of the methods in chapter 1.

Coconut-Papaya Ice

Welcome to the tropics! If you have the foresight to stock up and freeze papaya puree when it's available, this is a great sorbet to spring on your guests to cure the mid-winter blahs.

Garnish this sorbet with slices of sweet star fruit and serve it as a opener or during cocktails.

2 cups chopped fresh papaya (or 1½ cups frozen puree)
½ cup fresh orange juice
1½ cups coconut milk
¼ cup fresh lime juice
1 egg white, beaten until stiff
Sliced star fruit to garnish (optional)

Yield: 6 servings
Color: Yellow

Combine the papaya with the orange juice and puree in a food processor or blender. Strain the mixture through a fine sieve. Combine the papaya puree, coconut milk, and lime juice. Freeze according to one of the methods in chapter 1.

When the ice has frozen to a soft, slushy consistency, fold in the beaten egg white with a rubber spatula. Continue the freezing process until the ice is no longer slushy and has a firm texture. Garnish with sliced star fruit.

Note: To prepare coconut milk, pierce the eyes of a fresh coconut, drain, and reserve the liquid. Place the coconut on a hard surface, eyes down, and crack open with a hammer. Remove the coconut from the shell and coarsely grate. Put the grated coconut in a deep bowl and pour the reserved coconut liquid on top. Add 2 cups of boiling water and steep for about 1 hour. Strain the coconut through a fine sieve, pressing with the back of a large spoon to extract all the liquid. Discard the coconut meat. Chill the coconut milk until ready to use.

Variation

Coconut Mango Ice. Substitute 1½ cups mango puree for the papaya and proceed with the recipe as above.

Piña Colada Ice

This cool tropical delight can be made all year-round. The blend of coconut and pineapple makes this palate cleanser a nice first course sorbet.

2½ cups chopped pineapple (1 medium-size pineapple)
½ cup unsweetened grated coconut
1 cup coconut milk (see note, page 136)
⅓ cup fresh lime juice
1 tablespoon grated lime peel

Yield: 6 servings
Color: Pale yellow

Combine the pineapple and grated coconut and puree in a food processor or blender. Strain through a fine sieve and discard the solids. Combine the pineapple-coconut liquid with the coconut milk, lime juice, and peel. Freeze according to one of the methods in chapter 1.

Pineapple Cilantro Ice

The sweet, musky fragrance of fresh cilantro is nicely contrasted by the fresh pineapple and lime. Since cilantro is widely used in Mexican and Indian cuisines, this sorbet works well to complement some of those spicy dishes.

3 cups fresh pineapple chunks (1 medium-size pineapple)
¼ cup minced fresh cilantro (also known as fresh coriander and Chinese parsley)
¾ cup lime-flavored mineral water
⅓ cup fresh lime juice

Yield: 6 servings
Color: Yellow with green specks

Combine the pineapple, cilantro, mineral water, and lime juice in a blender or food processor and puree until smooth. Strain the mixture. Freeze according to one of the methods in chapter 1.

Prickly Pear-Banana Ice

The sweet watermelon smell of the prickly pear combined with the orange juice and banana makes this particular ice a delightful low-calorie frozen snack.

6 prickly pears
1 ripe banana
1 cup fresh orange juice
⅓ cup fresh lime juice

Yield: 6 servings
Color: Pink

Halve the prickly pears, scoop out the pulp, and reserve. Puree the banana with the orange juice in a food processor or blender. Combine the prickly pear pulp, banana-orange mixture, and the lime juice. Freeze according to one of the methods in chapter 1.

Papaya-Passion Fruit Ice

The combination of papaya and passion fruit makes this the most intensely flavored ice in this section. And by simmering the seeds and pulp of the passion fruit in orange juice, you will extract more flavor.

4 to 5 wrinkled passion fruit (or substitute ½ cup unsweetened passion fruit puree or ¾ cup unsweetened bottled passion fruit juice and reduce the quantity of orange juice to ¼ cup)
½ cup fresh orange juice
4 cups chopped fresh papaya (about 3 medium-size papayas)
½ cup water
¼ cup fresh lime juice

Yield: 6 servings
Color: Yellow

Over a noncorrosive saucepan, halve the passion fruit and scoop the juice, pulp, and seeds into the saucepan. Then add the orange juice and simmer over low heat for 25 to 30 minutes. Remove from the heat and cool. Strain the mixture and reserve.

Puree the papaya with the water in a blender or food processor and strain through a fine sieve. Combine the passion fruit mixture, the papaya puree, and lime juice. Freeze according to one of the methods in chapter 1.

Variation

Mango Passion Fruit Ice. Substitute 4 cups chopped fresh mango for the papaya and proceed with the recipe as above.

141

Chamomile Ice

Use this recipe as the basis for making ices with different teas. You can substitute raspberries for strawberries and pineapple or grape juice for orange. Mint and most fruit teas also work well in this combination. This ice fits in nicely between hardy soups, such as lentil or black bean, and a main course.

12 fresh strawberries
1 cup strong chamomile tea, chilled
1 cup fresh orange juice
1 egg white, beaten until stiff
Fresh strawberries slices and 1 tablespoon grated orange peel to garnish

Yield: 6 servings
Color: Pale orange

Puree the strawberries in a food processor or blender and strain through a fine sieve. Combine the strawberry puree, tea, and orange juice. Freeze according to one of the methods in chapter 1.

When the ice has frozen to a soft, slushy consistency, fold in the beaten egg white with a rubber spatula. Continue the freezing process until the ice is no longer slushy and has a firm texture.

Garnish with fresh strawberry slices and orange peel.

7
INTERNATIONAL ICES

Many cuisines have developed ways to cool the effects of their various dishes, spicy or otherwise. In Italy, besides *gelato* and *sorbetto*, a grainy textured ice called *granita* is served. *Dondurmas* are intensely flavored ices from Turkey. *Sharbats*, from which the word sherbet is derived, are Asian coolers that are surprisingly similar to snow cones. Then there are *spooms* (French) or *spumas* (Italian), which look like extremely smooth sorbets.

The primary difference between a sorbet and a granita is texture. While sorbets are smooth and slushy, granitas, as their name translates from the Italian, are grainy. Some restaurants in Italy even have commercial granita machines that produce tiny squares, or grains, of ice right alongside their gelato and sorbetto machines. But you won't need an ice machine to make granitas. In fact, all you need is a flat 9-inch by 13-inch by 2-inch baking pan and a fork or spoon, or a food processor, or a blender. Granitas are extremely easy to make.

All of the sorbet recipes in this book can be easily converted to granitas. Proceed with the sorbet recipe up to the point of freezing and use one of the two following methods.

Baking Pan Method. Pour the finished recipe into a flat 9-inch by 13-inch by 2-inch baking pan, cover with plastic wrap, and let the mixture harden in the freezer compartment of your refrigerator for about 4 hours. To serve, scrape the frozen mixture with a fork or spoon to create shavings. Serve in chilled bowls and glasses.

Food Processor or Blender Method. Pour the finished recipe into 2 ice cube trays with dividers in place, cover with plastic wrap, and let the mixture harden in the freezer compartment of your refrigerator for about 4 hours. Process the frozen cubes in short pulses in a food processor or blender until the texture is grainy, not slushy. Serve in chilled bowls and glasses.

Granitas have some advantages over sorbets. Granitas do not need to be stirred at intervals, as do sorbets. Because they don't have as low a freezing point as sorbets, they need little or no sugar syrup; therefore, granitas can be a real plus for dieters. You can adjust the sugar content in your recipes according to taste. And when it comes to appearance, granitas sparkle like jewels.

There is some likelihood that the *sharbat*, the Middle Eastern and Asian version of the granita, is among the oldest forms of flavored ices. Depending on the region, the word sharbat is widely used to describe frozen desserts or icy beverages (melted sharbats). One form of sharbat consists of a fruit puree or liqueur that is combined with sugar and water cooked to form a fruit syrup. The fruit puree or juices, sugar, and water mixture is cooked to the soft ball stage (234° F. to 240° F.) and then drizzled hot over crushed or shaved ice to congeal it.

The easiest and most accurate way to see if the syrup has reached the soft ball stage is by using a candy thermometer. However, there is a another easy way to check the syrup without one. Take a tablespoon of syrup and drop it into a bowl of ice water. It should form a soft, pliable ball. If it's brittle or hard, you've cooked it too long and you've got to start over with fresh ingredients. If it is loose and thread-like, you haven't cooked it long enough, but you are still in the ball game. You may notice sugar crystals forming around the sides of the pot. They should be removed or dissolved into the solution by brushing down the sides with a pastry brush.

A word of caution: Use a long-handled noncorrosive pot with a smooth interior surface that's at least three times the volume of your syrup. The boiling syrup will rise and expand in volume. Boiling syrup burns and will cling to the skin, so you can't be too careful.

When serving sharbats, you may want to keep some freezer space available to keep a tray of serving bowls cold. While preparing your sharbats, immediately replace each finished bowl in the freezer to prevent melting. Also, you should not serve sharbats in glass that cannot withstand a sudden temperature change.

As a country, Turkey is said have one foot in Europe and the other in Asia. The Turkish ice, *dondurma*, reflects exactly that. It's a combination of an Asian sharbat and an Italian granita. A citrus dondurma, like a sharbat, will incorporate quite a bit of peel or fruit in the preparation of its syrup. But it's frozen solid and then served like a granita.

A *spoom* or *spuma* is a mousse-like ice into which a meringue (egg whites beaten with sugar) is incorporated during the freezing process. While the textures of granitas and sharbats are coarse and grainy, spooms are smooth and light. Traditionally, a spoom is made with wine or champagne and is served in wine goblets. For a special presentation, you can pipe your spoom though a pastry bag fitted with a open star tip into your serving bowls.

Apple Cider Granita

Rosemary Gaitan, head pastry chef of Foley's Grand Ohio Restaurant in Chicago, serves this ice as both a palate cleanser and a dessert. This granita is perfect in a winter dinner following roast veal.

2¼ cups water
¾ cup sugar
Juice of 1 lemon
Pinch salt
4 cups apple cider
3 cups dry champagne
¼ cup (2 ounces) calvados
Fresh mint to garnish

Yield: 8 to 10 servings
Color: Tan

Make a syrup by combining the water and sugar in a noncorrosive saucepan and bring to a boil. Stir in the lemon juice and salt. Simmer for 5 minutes. Whisk together the syrup, cider, champagne, and calvados. Pour into two 8-inch by 8-inch cake pans and cover with plastic wrap. Freeze until the mixture is set, about 4 hours.

To serve, scrape the granita with a spoon or fork to create small shavings. Mound the shavings in glass dessert bowls or crystal champagne-daiquiri glasses and garnish with sprigs of fresh mint.

Chardonnay Granita

This granita really brings out the "oaky" vanilla flavor of California Chardonnays. This granita should be served in chilled wine goblets with a sprig of mint for a garnish.

½ **cup water**
¼ **cup sugar**
1 (750 ml) bottle California or
   Washington State Chardonnay
¼ **cup fresh lemon juice**
½ **teaspoon pure vanilla extract**

Yield: 8 servings
Color: Tan

Make a syrup by combining the water and sugar in a noncorrosive saucepan and bring to a boil. Simmer for 5 minutes. Cool the syrup and combine with the Chardonnay, lemon juice, and vanilla. Pour into two 8-inch by 8-inch by 2-inch cake pans and cover with plastic wrap. Freeze until the mixture is set, about 4 hours.

To serve, scrape the granita with a spoon or fork to create small shavings and spoon into individual chilled wine glasses. Keep the glasses in the freezer until ready to serve.

Raspberry Granita

There is a running argument in Italy between sorbetto and granita aficionados as to which is the better ice. The granita enthusiasts lay claim that theirs is superior because, in most cases, granitas are made with pure undiluted fruit. It's hard to argue with that, especially after you've had a spoonful of this raspberry granita. The raspberry and orange strike up a wonderful duet that will have your guests saying, "Bravo!"

2½ pints fresh raspberries
1 cup fresh orange juice
1 tablespoon grated orange peel
¼ cup fresh lemon juice

Yield: 6 servings
Color: Red

Puree the raspberries in a blender or food processor and strain to remove the seeds. Combine the raspberry puree, orange juice and peel, and lemon juice. Pour into a 9-inch by 13-inch by 2-inch cake pan and cover with plastic wrap. Freeze until the mixture is set, about 4 hours.

To serve, scrape the granita with a spoon or fork to create small shavings and spoon into individual chilled wine glasses or dessert bowls.

Granité Vin Rouge

At Philadelphia's classic French restaurant, Le Bec Fin, Premier Chef George Perrier serves this delicious ice between courses. A good full-bodied red wine is necessary for this granita, and Perrier suggests a Chateaunuef du Pape.

1 cup water
1 cup sugar
1 (750 ml) bottle Chateaunuef du Pape
or other full-bodied red wine
Juice of 1 orange
Juice of 1 lemon

Yield: 8 to 10 servings
Color: Burgundy red

Make a syrup by combining the water and sugar in a noncorrosive saucepan and bring to a boil. Simmer for 5 minutes. Remove the syrup from the heat and cool. Combine the syrup, wine, orange juice, and lemon juice and pour into two 8-inch by 8-inch cake pans. Cover with plastic wrap. Freeze until the mixture is set, about 4 hours.

To serve, scrape the granita with a spoon or fork to create small shavings and spoon into individual chilled wine glasses.

Herb Tea Granita

The combination of different teas in this recipe creates a variety of taste sensations. The mint tea cools the palate, while the Red Zinger and herbal teas provide depth for this ice.

4 cups water
¼ cup sugar
2 tea bags Red Zinger tea
2 tea bags Mo's Herbal tea (Celestial Seasons) or herbal tea of your choice
3 tea bags mint tea
Juice of ½ lemon
1 teaspoon grated lemon peel
Mint leaves to garnish

Yield: 6 servings
Color: Red

Make a syrup by combining the water and sugar in a noncorrosive saucepan, bring to a boil. Simmer for 5 minutes. Remove the syrup from the heat, add the tea bags, and steep, covered, for 10 to 15 minutes. Strain the tea or remove the tea bags and let the mixture cool. When the mixture has cooled, add the lemon juice and grated peel. Pour into a 9-inch by 13-inch by 2-inch cake pan. Freeze until the mixture has set, about 4 hours.

To serve, scrape the frozen granita with a spoon or a fork and place the shavings into chilled wine goblets. Keep the goblets in the freezer until you are ready to serve. Garnish with mint leaves.

Espresso Granita

At the close of a long dinner, espresso arrives in demitasse cups with a peel of lemon. Anyone who's savored that finale will really enjoy this ice. For added flavor, you can pour a tablespoon of Sambucca over each individual serving. Then serve.

For a rich dessert that looks like a frozen cappucino, top the Espresso Granita with the White Chocolate Sorbet minus the chocolate chips (page 114).

1 lemon
2 cups extra strong freshly brewed
  espresso
1 cup good quality freshly brewed coffee
1 cup water
⅓ cup sugar
Julienned lemon peel to garnish

Yield: 6 servings
Color: Light brown

Wash the lemon and peel. Make sure the white pith is removed or the ice will be bitter. Combine the espresso and the regular coffee, add the lemon peel, and steep for about 20 minutes. Strain the espresso/coffee to remove the peel.

Make a syrup by combining the water and sugar in a noncorrosive saucepan and bring to a boil. Simmer for 5 minutes. Remove the syrup from the heat and cool.

Juice the lemon and combine with the coffee and syrup. Pour into a 9-inch by 13-inch by 2-inch cake pan and cover with plastic wrap. Freeze until the mixture is set, about 4 hours.

To serve, scrape the granita with a spoon or fork to create small shavings and spoon into individual chilled dessert bowls. Garnish with the julienned lemon peel.

South Philly Italian Water Ice

Italian water ice is a direct descendent of sorbettos (Italy's sorbets), which came over with the Italian immigrants around the turn of the century. During the summer, vendors of water ice surface in front of row homes; they appear in the side windows of corner grocery stores. Most of the flavors are now made from commercially prepared syrups. But the intensely tart lemon water ice is still made from scratch, and there's bitter rivalries among water ice makers as to who is the best.

2 cups water
2 cups sugar
1½ cups fresh lemon juice
Julienned peel of 2 lemons

Yield: 8 servings
Color: White

Make a syrup by combining the water and sugar in a noncorrosive saucepan and bring to a boil. Simmer for 5 minutes. Combine the syrup, lemon juice, and lemon peel. Pour into a 9-inch by 13-inch by 2-inch cake pan and cover with plastic wrap. Freeze until the mixture is set, about 4 hours.

To serve, scoop the water ice with a spoon. Although the water ice freezes to a solid block, it will turn slushy when you serve it.

White Wine Spoom

California and Washington State Gewürtz-traminer wines are good choices for this spoom because of their very spicy citrus taste, which is further highlighted by the canned litchi nuts.

1 cup water
½ cup sugar
1 teaspoon brandy
Juice of 1 lemon
Juice of 1 lime
2 cups Chateau St. Jean Gewürtztraminer (or any wine of this type from California or Washington State)
3 egg whites
¼ cup confectioners' sugar
1 cup canned litchi nuts, halved

Yield: 8 servings
Color: Ivory

Make a syrup by combining the water, sugar, brandy, lemon juice, and lime juice in a noncorrosive saucepan and bring to a boil. Simmer for 5 minutes. Cool the syrup and combine with the wine. Freeze according to one of the methods in chapter 1, freezing it firmer than you would a sorbet.

To serve, make a meringue by beating the egg whites until soft peaks form, add the confectioners' sugar, and continue beating the eggs until the peaks are firm and shiny. Fold the meringue into the spoom. Fill a pastry bag fitted with a large star tip with the spoom and pipe into individual wine goblets. Garnish with litchi nuts.

Variations

Pear Wine Spoom. Substitute Paul Thomas Bartlett Pear Wine (or any of your own choosing) for the Gewürztraminer. Substitute Poire William or pear schnapps for the brandy and canned pear slices for the litchis. Proceed with the recipe as above.

Strawberry Beaujolais Spoom. Substitute a young (preferably a nouveau) Beaujolais for the Gewürztraminer, crème de cassis for the brandy, a cup of frozen strawberry puree for the water, and mandarin orange slices for the litchis. Proceed with the recipe as above.

Champagne Spoom. Substitute pink champagne for the Gewürztraminer. Proceed with the recipe as above.

Mango Sharbat

In this Indian version of sharbat, fresh fruit is tossed with sugar, frozen, and then served as either a slushy beverage or as an ice after a curry-laced meal. You're not limited to mango; any combination of fresh fruit and melon can be used.

4 to 5 cups finely chopped mango
½ cup sugar
¼ cup fresh lime juice
½ cup fresh orange juice
Fresh mint to garnish

Yield: 6 servings
Color: Yellow

Toss the mango cubes with the sugar and lime juice in a plastic bag. Seal and freeze the sugar-coated mango cubes for at least 4 hours. Combine the frozen mango cubes with the orange juice in a food processor or blender and puree for desired consistency: 1 to 2 minutes for coarse texture; 3 to 4 minutes for a smoother texture. Serve in wine glasses, garnished with fresh mint.

Variation

Melon Sharbat. Substitute 4 to 5 cups of either watermelon, cantaloupe, or honeydew melon (or any combination of the three), for the mangoes. Substitute fresh lemon juice for the lime juice and water for the orange juice. Proceed with the recipe as above.

Sour Cherry Sharbat

With this version of sharbat, sour cherries are incorporated into the syrup and drizzled over shaved ice. Does this procedure sound familiar? It should; its American cousin, the cherry snow cone is made practically the same way.

2½ cups pitted sour cherries
1½ cups water
Approximately 1½ cups sugar
4 tablespoons fresh lemon juice
6 individual serving bowls of shaved or crushed ice

Yield: 6 servings
Color: Red

Combine the cherries and water in a non-corrosive saucepan and bring to a boil. Simmer over low heat for 25 minutes. Strain the cherry mixture through fine sieve lined with a damp cheesecloth. Squeeze as much juice as you can from the cherries by pressing the fruit with the back of a spoon.

Measure the cherry juice and combine with an equal amount of sugar to make a syrup. Return the mixture to the saucepan, bring to a boil, and reduce to ¾ cup. Add the lemon juice. Immediately drizzle the hot syrup over the crushed ice or let the syrup cool, and then add it to the ice. Serve at once.

Orange Dondurma

Turkish dondurmas are the most intensely flavored citrus ices I've ever tasted. This intense flavor is developed as the lemon and orange peels are boiled with the syrup during the cooking stage, then steeped in the syrup for about an hour. The ice is different from granitas because of the way dondurmas incorporate fruit into their syrup.

3 whole juice oranges
1 whole lemon
3 cups water
1 cup sugar

Yield: 6 servings
Color: Light yellow

Wash the oranges and lemon and peel. (Make sure the white pith is removed from the peels or the ice will be bitter.) Combine the orange and lemon peels with the water in a noncorrosive saucepan and boil for 15 to 20 minutes. Remove from the heat and let the mixture steep for about an hour. Drain, discard the peel. Combine the liquid with the sugar in a saucepan and bring to a boil. Simmer for 5 minutes. Remove from the heat and cool. Juice the oranges and lemon and combine with the cooled mixture. Pour into a 9-inch by 13-inch by 2-inch cake pan and cover with plastic wrap. Freeze until set.

To serve, scrape the dondurma with a spoon or fork to create small shavings and spoon into individual chilled dessert bowls.

8

SERVING IDEAS, GARNISHES, AND SAUCES

Sorbets offer beautiful presentation possibilities. Their brilliant neon colors and soft pastels make it easy to create eye-catching arrangements. Sorbets can be sculpted into shapes, garnished with fresh fruit and fruit sauces, or they can be served in cups you can eat.

The secret of successful sorbet presentations is working quickly. Timing is important. If you are serving ices for a dinner party of 6 to 8 people, you have only a few minutes to work with each sorbet serving before the ices start to soften or melt. But by thinking through your visual ideas in advance and planning ahead, you can pull off stunning arrangements. A good rule of thumb about garnishing is that the garnish should be a supportive element, never overshadowing the item it's suppose to highlight.

Before you start, make sure you have ample room in the freezer compartment of your refrigerator for chilling the serving glasses or bowls. You'll also need some space to store your sorbets should you be forming them in advance. The refrigerator itself is a good place to store serving plates that have been sauced or garnished with sliced fruit or salads. The whole idea is to make the last-minute assembly as effortless and speedy as possible.

Shaping and Serving Ices

Traditionally, sorbets are formed into oval-shaped scoops. What you'll need are two large soup spoons (or tablespoons, if you want smaller portions) and a tumbler of cold water in which to dip the spoons between servings. This is a two-hand operation: one hand holds a spoon as it scoops the ice, while the other hand holds a spoon that shapes the top. Do only a few at a time and quickly place the shaped ices into a flat container, cover, and return the ices to your freezer until serving time. Instead of making oval shapes, you can use a melon baller to create grape-like clusters of multi-colored sorbets that really look wonderful when served in chilled wine goblets or tulip cookie cups garnished with sprigs of mint.

Sorbets from molds can make dramatic presentations. You can alternate different sorbet flavors and colors in bombe molds. By using round cake pans or loaf pans, you can serve wedges or slices of sorbet—which look especially nice in pools of colorful fruit sauces. You can also make individual servings by using small brioche or tart pans, ramekins, or petit fours molds, as well as savarin or baba au rhum molds. No matter what your choice of mold, the technique for storing and unmolding ices is pretty much the same.

To store, fill the mold with freshly made sorbet and cover tightly with plastic wrap. Store the mold with a serving plate (onto which you can invert your ices at serving time) for at least an hour in the freezer. To unmold, remove the mold from the freezer and invert over the cold serving plate. Dip a cloth in hot water, wring it out, and place the cloth over the mold for about 30 seconds. Give the mold and the plate a good shake, carefully remove the mold, and serve. When working with individual molds, remove each mold from the freezer one at a time, unmold, and immediately return each serving to the freezer as you finish.

Serving Dishes. Champagne saucers, wine glasses and goblets, decorative bowls and plates—your possibilities are limited only by your stock and wares. Prechilling your serving bowls and glasses is essential. You can also frost the rims of bowls and glasses by dipping the rims first in beaten egg whites and then in sugar before chilling.

Another way to serve sorbets is in containers that you actually eat. Almond or hazelnut tuiles or tulip cookie cups are simply elegant variations of ice cream cones.

Brandy snap baskets, chocolate cups, and meringue shells brimming with colorful ices make exquisitely flavored presentations. Recipes appear later in the chapter.

Garnishes and Sauces

Wild streaks of bright red raspberry sauce over a pool of sunshine yellow mango puree, confetti streamers of lime zest, or fanning slices of soft white pears with green mint leaves—these are just a few of the colorful fireworks that fruit garnishes can ignite. With candied citrus peels and a sharp knife you can accent sorbets with colored diamond shaped garnishes. Even something as simple and tasteful as a couple of fresh berries, a slice of kiwi, or a twist of lemon added to a sorbet is like adding sparkle to a ruby.

Savory sorbets can be garnished with tomato "roses" and sprigs of parsley or other fresh herbs. With a vegetable peeler you can create carrot curls and knots that add

that much more color to your ices.

Not only can you use fruits and vegetables as garnishes, but you can serve sorbets in them as well. Any thick-skinned fruit, such as oranges and lemons, as well as tomatoes and tamarillos, can be hollowed out and filled with sorbets piped from a pastry bag. Avocado and papaya halves stuffed with sorbets scooped with a melon baller make a grand entrance as a first course.

A fruit compote, which is fruit poached in wine, spirits, or syrup (or any combination thereof), combined on a plate with fruit sorbet can be a stunning creation of taste, texture, and color. First, set up individual plates by piping a shape or border with sieved strawberry, red currant, or apricot jam. Next, sauce the inside of the border with a smooth fruit puree or sauce, and then arrange on top your compote and sorbets. A sugarless version can be created with unsweetened fruit purees, a diced fruit coulis, and pure fruit ices from chapter 6.

Different colored fruit sauces, such as raspberry (red), papaya (yellow), and kiwi (green) can be piped across dessert plates to create electric patterns on which you can line up fanned sliced fruit and their sorbets.

Feathering sauces is an easy way to create swirling sun-bursting colors on your plate. The effect works the best with 2 sauces of different colors, such as a papaya (yellow) sauce and a raspberry (red) sauce. To sauce a plate, pour about ¼ cup of papaya sauce and gently tilt the plate back and forth until the sauce covers the surface. Next pipe on concentric circles or 3 to 4 parallel lines of raspberry sauce. To get a feathering effect, draw a skewer through the circles in a back-and-forth motion or swirl the skewer through the parallel lines.

When using fruit sauces, you will only need 4 to 6 tablespoons per serving (about ¼ cup or more depending on the size of the saucer or plate). Gently heating fruit sauces for 7 to 8 minutes will develop their flavor and make them sweeter without the addition of sugar. But be absolutely sure the sauce is refrigerator cool before adding your ices!

Here are some easy fruit sauces to start you on your way. The method is quite simple. Simply puree the fruit in a food mill, food processor, or blender until smooth. Then strain the puree to remove seeds, skins, and fibers. Then measure out the specified amount of puree. Since you won't be freezing these sauces as sorbets, the sugar syrup in these recipes can be adjusted to your taste and to the sweetness of the fruit. You can also substitute light corn syrup for sugar syrup. You can add melted jams and jellies and even fruit brandies or liqueurs to give your sauces added flavor depth. You can also substitute equal portions of frozen or canned fruits if fresh fruit is not available. Since frozen or canned fruit is usually presweetened, adjust the recipe with fresh lemon juice to taste.

Apricot Sauce (Yellow). Combine and simmer together 1½ cups strained apricot puree, 2 tablespoons lemon juice, and 1 tablespoon apricot brandy. Sweeten to taste with syrup or melted apricot jam.

Papaya Sauce (Yellow). Combine 1½ cups strained papaya puree and 2 tablespoons lime juice. Sweeten to taste.

Mango Sauce (Yellow). Combine 1½ cups strained mango puree and 2 tablespoons lime juice. Sweeten to taste.

Passion Fruit Sauce (Yellow). Combine and simmer together the pulp (including the seeds) of 4 passion fruit with 1 cup fresh orange juice. Sweeten to taste.

Lemon Sauce (Pale yellow). Combine and simmer together ⅓ cup lemon juice with 1 cup dessert wine or sweet champagne and 1 tablespoon light corn syrup.

Orange Sauce (Light yellow). Combine and simmer together 1½ cups fresh orange juice, julienned peel of 1 whole orange, and 2 tablespoons orange liqueur.

Cantaloupe Sauce (Orange). Sweeten to taste 1½ cups strained cantaloupe puree with syrup or melon or orange liqueur.

Watermelon Sauce (Pink). Sweeten 1½ cups strained watermelon puree to taste with syrup or crème de cassis.

Raspberry Sauce (Red). Combine 1½ cups strained raspberry puree with 1 tablespoon grated lemon peel and 2 tablespoons fresh lemon juice. Sweeten to taste with syrup, fruit brandy, or melted jam.

Strawberry Sauce (Red). Combine 1½ cups strained strawberry puree with 1 tablespoon grated orange peel and ¼ cup fresh orange juice. Sweeten to taste with syrup, fruit brandy, or melted jam.

Plum Sauce (Red). Simmer 2 cups coarsely chopped plums with ¼ cup sugar (at this stage you can flavor the mixture with diced fresh ginger, cardamom pods, or other seasonings of your choice). Remove from the heat, puree, and strain the mixture to remove skins.

Cranberry Sauce (Red). Simmer together 1½ cups fresh or frozen cranberries with ½ cup chopped fresh orange, 1 tablespoon grated orange peel, and ¼ cup sugar. Remove from the heat, puree, and strain.

Blueberry or Blackberry Sauce (Dark blue or purple). Combine 1½ cups strained berry puree with 1 tablespoon grated lemon peel and 2 tablespoons fresh lemon juice.

Honeydew Sauce (Light green). Sweeten 1½ cups strained melon puree to taste with sugar syrup or Midori or orange liqueur and add 2 tablespoons lime juice.

Kiwi Sauce (Light green). Combine 1½ cups strained kiwi puree and 2 tablespoons lemon juice and sweeten to taste.

To get the most mileage from garnishing, it's important to think with an eye for contrast. A mango sauce with a papaya sorbet will probably taste good but there won't be enough visual contrast between the two. Choose a sauce that is a different color than your sorbet for contrast or a different shade to create a toning effect. Remember that the colors of these sauces will, for the most part, be deeper and richer than their sorbet counterparts.

Some of the nicest garnishes are the simplest. And nothing can be simpler than garnishing sorbets with either candied citrus peel or flower petals. Candied citrus and flower petals can be made weeks in advance, and they are always great to have on hand to garnish any kind of dessert.

Candied Citrus Peel. Remove the peel from any citrus fruit and julienne into fine strips or shape with a paring knife into small diamonds or squares. (Be sure to remove the bitter tasting white pith.) In a noncorrosive heavy bottom saucepan, make a syrup by combining 1 cup sugar and ¼ cup water. Cook the syrup to an amber color, remove from the heat, and stir in the peel. After a few seconds, remove the peel with a slotted spoon and let dry on a baking rack.

Candied Flower Petals. Tiny rose buds and petals, violets, lilacs, and even mint and herb flowers are good choices for candied petals. Carefully remove the stems and leaves from the flowers and wash thoroughly before using.

The method used above for citrus peel works perfectly well with flowers, and you will get beautiful crystallized petals that can last almost indefinitely. The following quick method will give you finished petals that are softer and not as sweet as crystallized petals.

Stir 1 egg white with a fork until frothy. With a fine paintbrush, coat the petals on all sides and dust with superfine sugar. Place on a rack to dry.

Spun Sugar Nests. Placing richly colored ices on beautiful golden spun sugar nests will trigger ecstatic gasps when you serve them. It's as though you are mounting brightly colored jewels onto gold settings. And it's a great way to use leftover syrup from making candied citrus peels and flower petals.

In a noncorrosive heavy-bottom saucepan, make a syrup by combining 1 cup sugar and ¼ cup water. Cook the syrup to an amber color. Remove from the heat and place the saucepan over a bowl of cold water to prevent further cooking. Dip a fork into the syrup and spin the threads over a sheet of parchment paper in a circular motion to produce the nests. Center the nests on a individual dessert plates, add the sorbets, and serve.

Chocolate Shells. Chocolate shells are easy to make. Just brush melted chocolate into small brioche or tartlet molds, paper muffin cups (double thickness), and even small paper bags. You can also create a marbled effect by brushing the insides of molds with various combinations of white, milk, and semi-sweet (dark) chocolates. You'll need at least 2 ounces of chocolate per serving.

Tulip Cups

Also know as tuiles, these almond or hazel-nut cookies can be shaped into cups, cones, or cornets, and then filled with a sorbet to make a pleasing dessert presentation.

¼ **cup softened unsalted butter**
½ **cup confectioners' sugar**
¾ **teaspoon almond extract**
¼ **cup egg whites**
¼ **cup all-purpose flour**
⅓ **cup lightly toasted, coarsely chopped almonds or hazelnuts**

Yield: Approximately 16 tulip cups

Preheat the oven to 425° F. and line a bakery sheet with buttered parchment paper.

In a bowl, cream the butter. Beat in the confectioners' sugar until the mixture is smooth. Add the almond extract and egg whites and continue beating until smooth. Sift the all-purpose flour into the batter. Then fold in the nuts.

For each cookie, spoon 1½ tablespoons of batter onto the buttered baking sheet and bake in the preheated oven for 5 to 6 minutes or until the edges are light brown. Remove from the oven and let the cookies rest for 30 seconds. Quickly place the cookies in a cup or small brioche mold and shape with a small glass. Let the cups cool, then fill with sorbet.

Brandy Snap Baskets

¼ cup molasses
¼ cup unsalted butter
⅔ cup sugar
½ cup all-purpose flour
1 teaspoon ground ginger
½ teaspoon grated lemon peel
½ teaspoon fresh lemon juice
2 tablespoons brandy or cognac

Yield: Approximately 16 brandy snaps

Preheat the oven to 350° F. and line a bakery sheet with buttered parchment paper.

In a saucepan, gently heat the molasses, butter, and sugar until the butter has melted and the sugar has dissolved. Remove from the heat and stir in the flour, ginger, lemon peel, lemon juice, and brandy.

For each basket, spoon 1½ tablespoons of batter onto the buttered baking sheet. Spoon only 3 portions at a time. Bake in the preheated oven for 10 to 12 minutes or until the edges are light brown. Remove the baking sheet from the oven and quickly remove each snap with a frosting spatula and place in a cup or small brioche mold and shape with a small glass. Cool before filling with sorbet.

Brandy snaps can also be shaped into cones or cornets.

Meringue Shells

Also known as vacherin shells, these make the sweetest and airiest containers imaginable. You can vary the flavor with chocolate and nuts as well.

4 egg whites
½ teaspoon cream or tartar
1 cup confectioners' sugar
½ teaspoon vanilla extract

Yield: 6 shells

Preheat the oven to 200° F. Butter 2 baking sheets and dust with all-purpose flour.

Beat the egg whites with the cream of tartar until the eggs form soft peaks. Gradually add ½ cup of the confectioners' sugar, 1 tablespoon at a time, and beat in the vanilla. When the whites form stiff shiny peaks, fold in the remaining ½ cup confectioners' sugar.

Fill a pastry bag fitted with a ½-inch plain round or large star tip and pipe the meringue into six 3-inch to 4-inch circles. After the circles are complete, pipe a rim with the meringue to the desired height (about 2 inches). Bake the meringues in an oven until they are a very light tan, 2 to 2½ hours. Remove the shells from the oven and cool completely before serving.

Index